NAPOLEON'S MEDALS

This book is number

000978

of a limited edition

of 1000 copies.

EN CHEF DE L'ARMÉE

OFFERT A L'INSTITUT NATION
PAR B. DUVIVIER
A PARIS

NAPOLEON'S MEDALS

VICTORY TO THE ARTS

RICHARD A. TODD

The History Press

First published 2009

The History Press
The Mill, Brimscombe Port
Stroud, Gloucestershire, GL5 2QG
www.thehistorypress.co.uk

© Richard A. Todd, 2009

The right of Richard A. Todd to be identified as the Author
of this work has been asserted in accordance with the
Copyrights, Designs and Patents Act 1988.

All rights reserved. No part of this book may be reprinted
or reproduced or utilised in any form or by any electronic,
mechanical or other means, now known or hereafter invented,
including photocopying and recording, or in any information
storage or retrieval system, without the permission in writing
from the Publishers.

British Library Cataloguing in Publication Data.
A catalogue record for this book is available from the British Library.

ISBN 978 0 7524 4999 9

Typesetting and origination by The History Press
Printed in Malta

Contents

	Abbreviations	6
	Acknowledgements	7
	Introduction	8
I	'Victory to the Arts'	9
II	Napoleon and his Engravers	28
III	Bonaparte – God and Hero	40
IV	Conquest of Nature	50
V	First Italian Campaign	71
VI	Egypt	78
VII	First Consul	84
VIII	14 July 1800	88
IX	England – Peace and War	96
X	Napoleon – Emperor and King	107
XI	Austerlitz and Aftermath	115
XII	Prussia	127
XIII	Austria	140
XIV	The Face of History	147
XV	The Family	161
XVI	The Royal Marriage	168
XVII	The King of Rome	174
XVIII	Star of Destiny	183
XIX	The Hundred Days	201
XX	The Legend	212
	Bibliography	218
	Index of Medals	220
	Index	223

Abbreviations

BR   L. Bramsen, *Médaillier Napoléon le Grand*, Hamburg: 1977 (reprint).

H   M. Hennin, *Histoire numismatique de la révolution française*, Paris, 1826.

Trésor   George-Julian Fellmann and M. Charles Lormant, *Trésor de numismatique et de glyptique*, Paris, 1836 and 1840.

Essling   *Importante collection de monnaies et médailles*, Paris, 1927. (Sale of Prince Essling's Collection.)

Edwards   Edward Edwards, ed. *The Napoleon Medals*. London, 1837. (First volume of the *Trésor*.)

AN   *Vivant Denon, Directeur des Musées sous le Consulat et L'Empire. Letters to Napoleon.*

Corresp.   *Correspondence de Napoléon*, 32 volumes, Paris, 1858–1870. Published by order of Napoleon III.

In all of the attributions, the first name is that of the artist/designer, the second that of the engraver.

Acknowledgements

I would like to thank all of those who have helped bring this book to a successful conclusion. First of all, Jim Crawley and Shaun Barrington of The History Press, who first saw the possibilities for publication in my photographs of the Napoleon medals. The Inter-Library Loan department of the Wichita State University found books for me that I hardly knew existed, including the complete files of *Le Moniteur,* Henin's *Histoire Numismatique de la Révolution Française,* and three articles in *The Medal* by Antony Griffiths, which transformed my understanding of the production of the medals.

I would like to thank also all those from whom I have purchased medals over the years, in particular Seaby's of London and one dealer in rare coins in California, Karl Stephens, who frequently found for me the exact medal I needed at a critical moment in my research. Then there were the three members of Douglas Photographic Imaging, Rick, Nancy, and Penny, who struggled with me over the years to construct from my negatives just the right images in colour, shading and contrast, and of course provided the final transfer of pictures electronically to the publisher. Without them this book would not have been possible. It is important to remember that the medals and coins in this volume are not reproduced to scale. It was felt that the provision of the maximum detail was more useful to the reader than the representation of relative size. In order to avoid constant page references in the text, an index to the images is provided on page 220.

Finally, I wish to thank my wife, Barbara, for countless hours spent proof reading and otherwise correcting my errors and my son, Geoffrey, for his computer skills and sage advice. I bear responsibility for those mistakes that still remain.

Richard A. Todd

Introduction

Antony Griffiths wrote of the medallions of the Napoleonic era: 'What impressed me was the extraordinary quality of the design and craftsmanship of the medals, which seem to me to be some of the masterpieces of French neoclassical art.' What needs also to be said is that these superb works of art and craftsmanship were used creatively in the service of the 'hero' of that age with a skill unequalled before or since. When that image was abandoned, as it was for Louis XVIII, or tampered with, as for Louis Philippe – the magic was gone.

These works of art and propaganda have never been published adequately. Most of them have never been seen, even in monochrome reproduction, except by a few scholars and collectors. The reproductions that do exist, aside from a few examples in specialized articles and monographs, are in early nineteenth-century catalogues and twentieth-century auction lists. Within the last few years, two websites have appeared with medals scanned in colour, but these, though welcome, are subject to the limitations of both access and quality.

As for commentary, there are some in the nineteenth-century catalogues and useful notes by the late David Block on the website, *fortiter*. There are biographies of Vivant Denon, but these deal with Denon's more spectacular achievements as Napoleon's Director of Public Works.

Important articles dealing with certain aspects of the Napoleonic medals themselves are by Antony Griffiths and Catherine Delmas. Bramsen's *Médaillier Napoléon le Grand*, with a nearly complete listing of the medals, has become the standard reference work but it lacks both commentary and illustration.

None of these works, though important for the study of Napoleon's medallions, displays them as 'the masterpieces of French neoclassical art', or integrates them into the life and history of Napoleon Bonaparte.

Napoleon's Medals: Victory to the Arts, not only calls attention to a neglected artistic achievement but also fills a void in the history of Art and Empire. This is not another history of Napoleon but a work of art history, showing how the medals illuminate every aspect of his reign. It shows how the ancient models and themes were used to clothe Napoleon with heroic, even divine, attributes in memorialising the grand events of his career.

I
'Victory to the Arts'

Among the most interesting in the series of Napoleonic medallions are those which deal with the acquisition of Italian works of art by the French armies. The French 'Committee of Scholars' and the medals themselves insist that the capture of the Italian treasures was a 'Victory to the Arts'. Not only were these masterpieces seen as legitimate spoils of war but their transportation to Paris – the new owners asserted – would advance the cause of art itself. Some of the more famous pieces are seen on the medals, affirming the greatness of France and of Bonaparte, and supporting his programmes.

On 16 August 1803, Napoleon visited the Louvre to view the celebrated Venus de Medici and received from Vivant Denon, Director General of Museums, a medal depicting the ancient masterpiece, 'without doubt the most beautiful work of art!' Denon insisted.[1] The Venus had only recently arrived from Palermo where she had been sent by the Florentines to escape the French Army – but in vain. The fugitive goddess, caught in the web of Tallyrand's skillful diplomacy, had been returned to Paris instead of Florence. (A British offer to keep her safe at Gibraltar had been rejected.) Writing to Napoleon on 14 July 1803, Denon was ecstatic: 'The Venus has finally arrived! ... *Jamais plus beau trophée de victoire!*'[2] The medal itself proclaims the victory: *AUX ARTS LA VICTOIRE.*

More than simply a prize of war, the arrival of the Venus was a 'victory for the arts' because only in Paris could great art be studied properly and only there was it safe.

> Today we can say ... that she [the Venus] is in the safe keeping of the most powerful of nations, and that the sanctuary where she is placed is for her the temple of Janus of which the doors are closed forever.[3]

VENUS DE MEDICI (1803). Greek masterpiece from Florence. First of Denon's medals presented to Napoleon on arrival of the sculpture at the Paris Museum. The inscription reads 'VICTORY TO THE ARTS'. (Jeuffroy; Br. 280).

NAPOLEON'S MEDALS: *Victory to the Arts*

Such excuses were hardly necessary for Denon, Bonaparte, and the French 'Committee of Scholars' to whom was assigned the collection of the best Italian art. The idea of art as a prize of war was an old one, but never was it embraced so enthusiastically, pursued with such thoroughness, or portrayed with such creativity as by the French government, its agents and its artists in the years of the Directory and the Consulate.

The abduction of art by French armies had begun as early as the Year II of the Republic, with the victories in the Low Countries, and continued under the Consulate and the Empire, but Napoleon's Italian Campaign was the climax of both effort and achievement. Napoleon, appointed commander of the Army of Italy in March 1786, shattered the Austrian Army in less than a year, and the Treaty of Campoformio of 17 October 1797 confirmed French control of northern Italy. Napoleon cooperated enthusiastically with the Commissioners of the Republic as together they stripped Italy of its art treasures. The most celebrated prizes were those acquired from Rome by the Treaty of Tolentino with the Vatican, signed in February of 1797.[4]

> The Committee of Scholars has reaped a good harvest at Ravenna, Rimini, Pesaro, Ancona, Loretto and Perugia. That will be sent immediately to Paris. Joined to what we shall be sending from Rome, we will have everything of beauty in Italy except for a few things at Turin and Naples.

How natural, therefore, that Bonaparte should appear as *ITALICUS* on a medal of 1797, struck for the Treaty of Campoformio at the end of the Italian Campaign. This Latin title places him in the ancient tradition of the triumphant Roman general returning with spoil, like Lucius Mummius, named '*Acaicus*' for his Greek victory in 146BC, and remembered for his shipments of Corinthian art back to Rome after the destruction of that city. Bonaparte was named for the country he had conquered and plundered.

If there is any justification for the theft of Italian art it is that an extensive programme was undertaken to introduce the French public to great art. Paintings and sculpture were sent out to fifteen provincial museums but were first exhibited in the Louvre for the general public. Nine of the exhibitions were held between 1799 and 1814.[5] There were also regular columns in *Le Moniteur* on the great artists and their works.

BONAPARTE AS ITALICUS (1797). Pewter, struck for the Treaty of Campoformio at the end of the First Italian Campaign, by an Italian tobacco dealer in Strasbourg. The title, *ITALICUS*, named for the conquered country, places Bonaparte in the tradition of other conquerors who were also plunderers. (H. 812).

'VICTORY TO THE ARTS'

A few voices were raised in protest at the removal of the Italian art treasures. Quatremere de Quincy was the author (in 1796) of an eloquent petition to the Directory, published in an extensive pamphlet, signed by eminent French artists, protesting the plunder and insisting that the Italian works could only be studied properly in their natural surroundings.[6] The signers of a counter-petition pointed out that the Romans themselves had first stolen the art from the Greeks and maintained that Paris was the only secure and suitable place for the study of great works of art.[7] It is not surprising to find as one of the signatories to the counter-petition Pierre Simon Benjamin Duvivier, engraver of the medal that appeared in April of 1798 in celebration of the acquisition of the Italian treasures, which had already left Rome, to arrive in Paris in July 1798.[8] Duvivier's medal shows a triumphant Bonaparte, holding an olive branch but led by a warlike Minerva, about to be crowned by a winged Victory. The legend on the medal, *PAIX SIGNEE L'AN 6. REP. FR.*, commemorates the Peace of Campoformio, but the real interest of the artist is clear, for the Victory who crowns Bonaparte with her right hand cradles in her left arm the Apollo Belvedere, most esteemed of the Vatican treasures – 'Victory to the arts!'

An inscription declares 'the arts and sciences grateful', as well they might be to the rapacious Commission and to the general who had made it all possible. The arts might have been disappointed that when the the treasures first arrived in Paris, most of them were still enclosed in their garlanded packing cases, as an engraving of the processions shows them.[9] Only the bronze-gilt horses taken from San Marco in Venice are visible, along with a pair of caged lions and four dromedarie – presumably appreciated by the sciences.

There is no disappointment, however, in De Concourt's enthusiastic description of the scene. 'The eternal city itself never saw so grand a spectacle, never did an emperor's victorious return passing through her proud streets trail behind such an army of such captives.'[10] *Le Moniteur*[11] compared the festival parade to the Triumph of Aemilius Paulus,[12] who returned with spoil from his victory over the Macedonian King Perseus, in 168BC. A banner carried before the third division of the parade proclaimed of the newly arrived treasures.

La Grèce les céda: Rome les a perdus:
Leur sort changea deux fois, il ne changera plus.

TREATY OF CAMPOFORMIO (1797). Really struck to celebrate the arrival of the Italian art in Paris, July 1798. The Victory who crowns Bonaparte holds in her arm the Apollo Belvedere, taken from the Vatican. 'THE SCIENCES AND THE ARTS GRATEFUL' reads the inscription. (Duvivier; H. 811), 56mm.

NAPOLEON'S MEDALS: *Victory to the Arts*

ARRIVAL OF THE ITALIAN TREASURES IN PARIS (July 1798). An old engraving shows the procession. Most of the works of art are still encased but some of the animals are visible. The bronze horses from St Mark's in Venice are in the foreground. (Charles Saunier, *Les Conquêtes Artistiques de la Révolution et de L'Empire,* Paris, 1902, Pl, IV)

The horses of St Mark's, *Le Moniteur* proclaimed, 'are finally on free soil!'

The scene was remembered and appears again on a Sèvres porcelain vase[13] with the horses from St Mark's, led by Roman soldiers, brought to life in the centre and the Apollo Belevdere, the Laocoon, and other famous pieces resurrected from their packing cases. Many Napoleonic designs, some directly from medals, appear on Sèvres porcelain in this period.

General Bonaparte, whose conquests had made the festival possible, was not present – he was beginning a new conquest in Egypt – more definitively a victory for the arts than his campaign in Italy, for his team of scientists and artists which surveyed the antiquities of the country later produced the monumental *Description de l'Egypt,* the foundation of modern Egyptology.

The gratitude of the arts and sciences, proclaimed on Duvivier's medal of 1797, found a fuller expression when the refurbished Central Museum of Art – where the Italian treasures were taken – was renamed *Musée Napoléon* in June 1803. The installation of the Apollo in its own gallery in the museum gave Bonaparte, now First Consul, an opportunity to show his admiration for the masterpiece and to once again assert the right of ownership though conquest.

In November of 1800, Bonaparte placed on the base of the Apollo Belvedere a bronze plaque.

'VICTORY TO THE ARTS'

The statue of Apollo, which stands on this pedestal found at Antium toward the end of the fifteenth century, placed in the Vatican by Julius the Second, at the commencement of the sixteenth century, was conquered in the fifth year of the Republic by the army of Italy, under the command of General Bonaparte … was placed here on the 21st Germinal in the year VII – the first year of his consulate.[14]

A pair of medals dated 1803, but actually struck in 1810,[15] shows the Apollo Belvedere and the Laocoon, the Hellenistic *tour de force* also taken from the Vatican, in the *Musée Napoléon*. Other Italian acquisitions may be recognised on the medals. On the right of the entrance to the Apollo Gallery is the Meleager, from the Vatican also, and on the right of the *Salle de Laocoon*, the Pallas (or Minerva) from Velletri, acquired in Italy in 1801.

The French passion to possess the symbols of ancient grandeur was enormous. Some trophies that could not be moved – such as the Arch of Septimius Severus

APOLLO AND LAOCOON GALLERIES (1804).
Musée Napoléon in the Louvre. The named statues may be seen at the end of each gallery. The Minerva from Velletri can be seen at the right front of the Laocoon Gallery. These medals were not struck until 1810. (Br. 370, 367)

13

NAPOLEON'S MEDALS: *Victory to the Arts*

and the Column of Trajan – were imitated. The copies naturally appeared on the medals, celebrating the artistic triumph of Napoleon's monumental building campaign. The Carrousel Arch is a copy of the triple arch of Septimius Severus in the Roman Forum. The Roman arch celebrates the victories of Severus' Parthian campaign; the Carrousel honours the victories of the Grand Army in the campaign of Austerlitz, the Entry into Vienna, the Entry into Munich, the Interview of the Two Emperors, and the Peace of Pressburg.[16]

The bronze-gilt horses from St Mark's were placed on top of the Carrousel Arch and may be seen on the medal. They pull a triumphal chariot led by two victories and bearing a statue of the Emperor by the sculptor Lamot. The medal, struck in 1806 as construction of the arch was just beginning, is in error. Vivant Denon, director of the project and of the Medal Mint, could not have known when he commissioned the design that Napoleon would order his statue removed from the chariot just after it was installed, as described by the architect Fontaine.

> His majesty replied angrily that he regarded that arrangement as a shameful thing … He ordered that his statue, which had already been elevated into the car, be taken down. 'It is not for me', he said, 'it is for others to make statues for me. Let the car with the Victories remain, but it will remain empty.'[17]

Both Napoleon and Fontaine protested ignorance of Denon's intention. Fontaine insisted that he was led to believe the figure in the chariot was to be that of Mars, the god of war. The statue would later be placed in the Orangerie.[18]

This apparent misfortune for Lamot's statue was its salvation however, for it escaped the vengeance of the Allies in 1815 when the two Victories and the chariot were thrown to the ground and demolished.[19] The bronze horses were removed by the Austrians and returned to St Mark's in Venice.

The French general Pommereul once proposed that another much admired ancient monument, the Column of Trajan in Rome, be dismantled and re-erected in Paris.[20] Fortunately, wiser counsel prevailed, but the column set up in Paris in honour of the Grand Army and the victories of the campaign of 1805 is a close imitation of Trajan's Dacian War memorial, though executed in bronze over a masonry core, rather than carved in marble.

CARROUSEL ARCH (1806). Copied from the Arch of Septimius Severus in the Roman Forum and dedicated to the Grand Army of 1805. The bronze horses from St Mark's in Venice have been placed on top. The medal is inaccurate in one respect; Napoleon modestly ordered his statue taken down. Fontaine also signed the medal as architect. (Brenet; Br. 557)

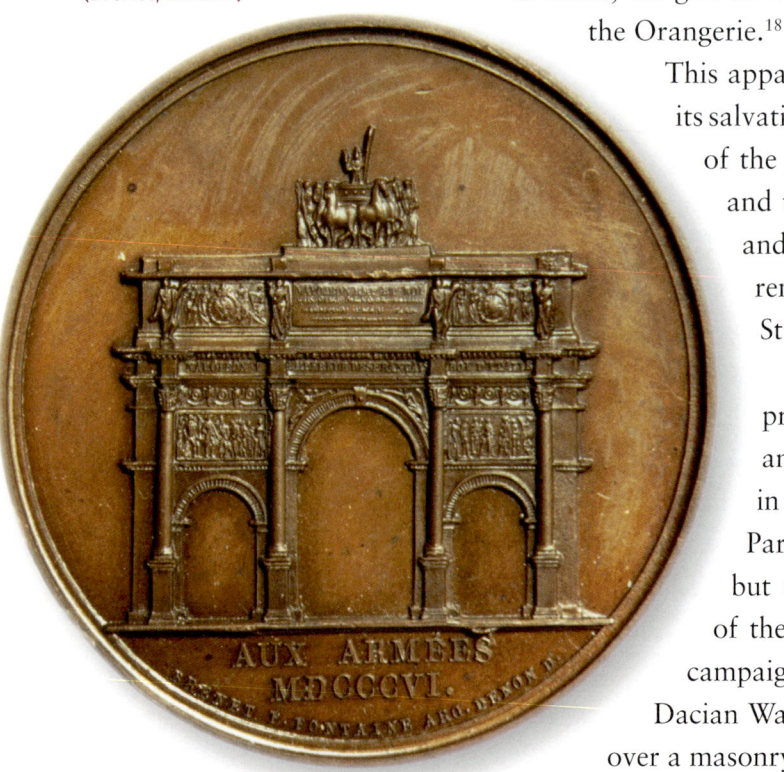

'VICTORY TO THE ARTS'

Another ancient monument used creatively by Napoleon's engravers was the Temple of Janus in the Roman Forum. In time of war the door of the ancient Temple was open, in time of peace closed. The temple no longer exists, but it survives on a well known bronze of Nero, which may be the model for two of Andrieu's medals, though Andrieu's temple is much more elaborate. For the Peace of Pressburg, which in 1805 ended the war with Austria, the medal shows the door closed (Br. 455). When the Austrians broke the peace in 1809, the violence of the act is shown by a representation of the same temple with the door, not open as the ancient convention dictated, but shattered, the pieces lying on the steps (Br. 844). Napoleon once proposed to Cambaceres the erection of his own temple of Janus on Montmarte, where would be made 'the first ceremonial proclamations of peace and the distribution of decennial prizes'.[21]

It was Vivant Denon's appointment as Director of Museums on 19 November 1802 and of the *Monnaie des Médailles* in September of 1803 that was decisive for the success of the *Histoire métallique,* Bonaparte's medallic history. Although

COLUMN OF THE GRAND ARMY (1805). A bronze column over a masonry core, erected in the *Place Vendôme* imitates the Column of Trajan in Rome. Chaudet's statue of Napoleon as Emperor stands at the top. The spiral relief of the French Campaign of 1805 parallels Trajan's pictorial description of his Dacian War. (Leperre; Brenet; Br. 463)

NAPOLEON'S MEDALS: *'Victory to the Arts'*

VIVANT DENON (1825). Medal struck at his death in 1825. Director of Museums and of the Medal Mint for most of Napoleon's reign, Denon was unofficially also his Director of the Arts and Public Works. A sly smile betrays his legendary wit. (Donadio)

a number of beautiful medals had been produced before Denon took charge, by N. Gatteaux, Duvivier, Brenet, and Andrieu, it was Denon's supervision that brought order and purpose to the series.

More than just administrative skill, it was the Director's personal attention to detail in the design of many of the medals that was decisive. This becomes apparent in his correspondence. Two examples show Denon's creativity in using the acquisition of Italian art to glorify Napoleon and his programme.

'The Pallas [Athena; Minerva] of Velletri has arrived!' Denon announced to Bonaparte on 7 December 1803.[22] Installed quickly in the Museum, like the Venus she merited a special visit from the First Consul and his wife on the 19th.[23] In the next year, the Pallas appeared on a medal assisting Napoleon in one of the most important achievements of his career, the publishing of the Civil Code (21 March 1804).

Denon's original idea, explained to Napoleon in a letter of December 1803,[24] was to place his portrait on the obverse, with oak leaves and a civic crown, and the Pallas on the reverse. Denon's habitual cleverness, however, conceived

'VICTORY TO THE ARTS'

a prettier conceit. The pose and the open hand of the Minerva from Velletri proved irresistible to the Director of the Medal Mint. In the Goddess' hand was placed a scroll, Napoleon's Civil Code. On the other face of the medallion stands Bonaparte, in classical dress, also holding the scroll of the Code, having received it from the Goddess of Wisdom.

GIVING OF THE CIVIL CODE (1804). When the Minerva from Velletri arrived in Paris from Italy, Denon immediately determined to use her in conjunction with a statue of Napoleon to celebrate the Civil Code. On this medal Napoleon receives the Code from Minerva, goddess of wisdom. The model for Napoleon was a statue by Chaudet set up in the Legislative Chamber. (Brenet; Br. 291)

NAPOLEON'S MEDALS: *'Victory to the Arts'*

LA VACCINE (1804). Venus de Medici supports Napoleon's smallpox vaccination programme, secure in the embrace of the physician-god Aesculapius. In the field is a cow, source of the vaccine, a hypodermic device to deliver it, and a tube containing the vaccine. A bandage (perhaps) on the goddess's left arm is proof of her personal endorsement. The medal was not actually produced until 1809 although the scene was conceived by Denon in 1806. (Andrieu; Br. 400)

Bonaparte's image is a copy of a marble statue by Chaudet, voted in gratitude to the new lawgiver by the Legislature and placed in the centre of their meeting hall.[25] Chaudet's statue was much admired when installed in January 1805. It was described in *Le Moniteur* as 'serious in character, as is the law, the idea of which it calls to mind; the security, the confidence which it seems to inspire.'[26] That Chaudet had succeeded in portraying the nobility of the Emperor Napoleon is proved by the fact that the head of the statue became the model for Andrieu's portrait that became the standard obverse type for the Empire.

The Venus de Medici makes a special appearance in support of Napoleon's vaccination programme for smallpox.[27] On January 25, 1806, in a letter to the Minister of the Interior,[28] Denon reported a request for the Ministry to produce a medal to commemorate the introduction of smallpox vaccination into France in the year 1800. The Ministry had suggested an uninteresting design, a head of the

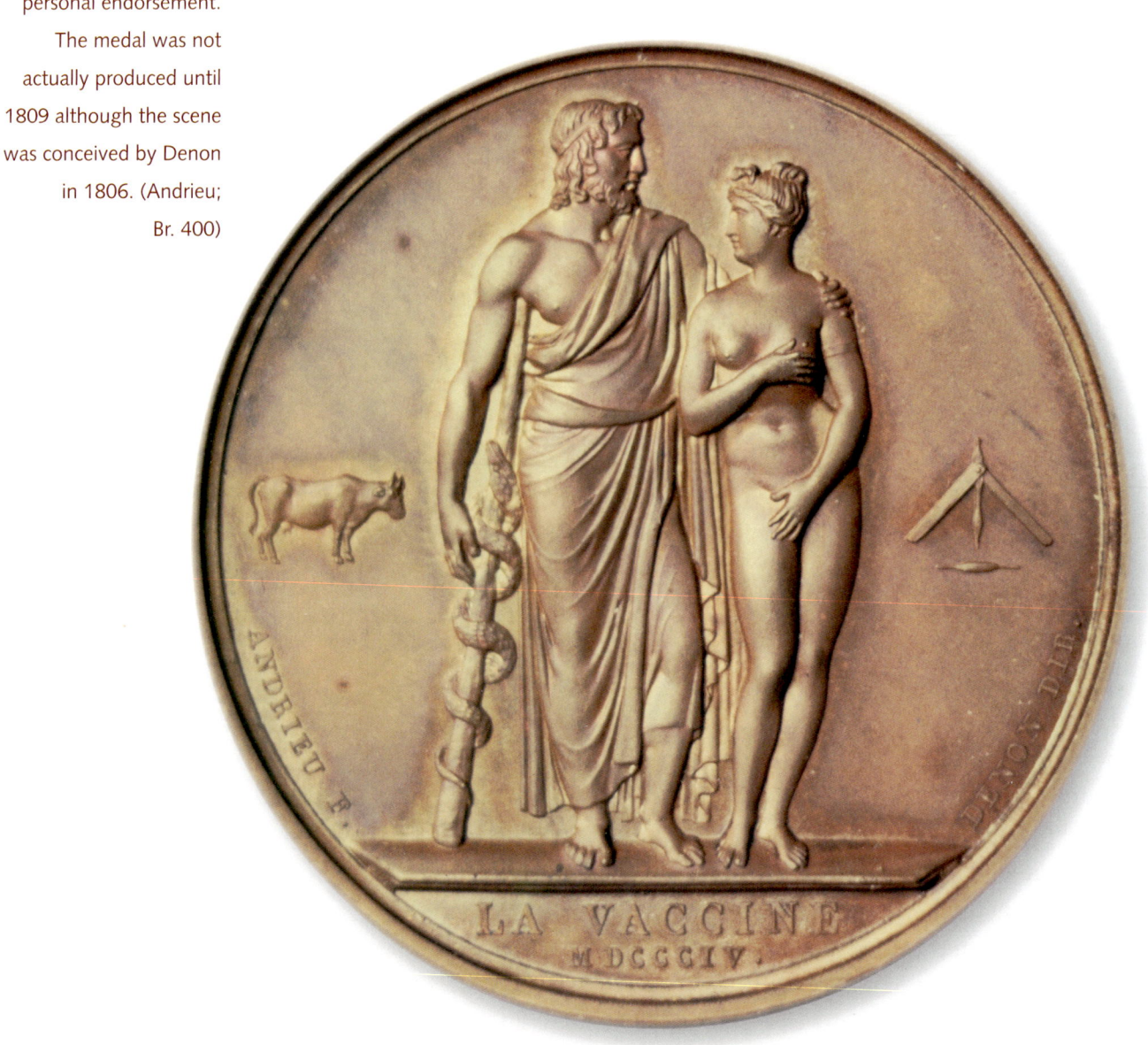

'VICTORY TO THE ARTS'

Emperor on the obverse, on the reverse an oak leaf wreath with an inscription. Denon's counter-proposal was another 'Victory to the Arts' and a reflection of the Mint Director's sly sense of humor. A cow, provider of the vaccine, would appear on one face of the medal, on the other, 'Aesculapius ministering to a beautiful woman with the features of the Venus de Medici'.

The sculptor, Chaudet – who did the statue of Napoleon for the legislative chamber and that on top of the Vendôme Column – was the natural choice to design the Venus for the engraver, Andrieu. Chaudet's design for this medal lacks the seriousness praised in the statue for the Legislature. It follows Denon's creative suggestions, except that the cow now shares the reverse with the Venus, the physician-god Aesculapius, a hypodermic delivery system, and a tube below it containing the vaccine. Secure in the embrace of her benefactor, the goddess smiles her gratitude.

It is tempting also to see, as do Bramsen, De Fayolle, and the *Trésor*,[29] a bandage on the left arm of the goddess, further proof of her personal endorsement. Examination of the statue itself, however, shows a bracelet on the

CONQUEST OF ILLYRIA (1809). Cow suckling her calf, copying a motif found on ancient Illyrian coins. Note the club of Hercules in the field, also found on the coins. Hercules is supposed to have performed deeds in the area of Illyria. Depaulis also produced the cow for the vaccination medal of the Paris municipalities. (Depaulis; Br. 879)

SILVER DRACHMAS OF ILLYRIAN CITIES (third to second centuries BC). The cow suckling her calf was a type borrowed by Denon for this medal – over the protest of Daru, Napoleon's Intendant of the Palace. Note the club of Hercules on the coin.

20

arm where the 'bandage' appears on the medal. It is quite possible, of course, that Andrieu, or Chaudet (or more likely Denon) transformed the bracelet into a bandage.

However that may be, the scene is successful, though in poor taste. A marble deity has been transformed into a flesh and blood woman. This is just the sort of irreverent trick that the brilliant and witty Denon, rationalist child of the Enlightenment and celebrated libertine, might play on a goddess. His tricks on other artists and collectors are legendary, like the Rembrandt etching he made for Sir William Hamilton,[30] which that knowledgeable collector later sold as an original. Twenty years later, on the medal struck at his death in 1825, Denon is still smiling (page 16).

An interesting exchange between Denon and Daru shows Denon's personal concern with the details of a medal and demonstrates how superior to Daru's insensitive criticism was the Director's insight. Denon has submitted the medal designs for the Austrian Campaign of 1809 to Napoleon, who by this time (January 1811) had assigned their approval to Daru, Intendant General of the Palace. Daru proceeds through the designs, carping at details. He says of the Illyrian medal, 'It is a cow. I confess that I find little nobility there.'[31]

Denon replies that since Illyria had come to France by treaty there was no obvious subject to picture on the medal. In that case one must go to the ancient coins of the country (the Illyrian drachmas). Denon offers to suspend production until he has found a better subject, but adds testily, 'If one comes to you, *Monsieur le Comte*, I would be obliged if you would communicate it to me.'

Our immediate response on viewing the medal, engraved as originally designed, is that if a cow is not a noble subject this is certainly a noble cow! The engraver, Depaulis, certainly endowed the beast with personality.

In 1814, the Municipalities of Paris struck a *jeton* to show that Paris also had adopted the medical advance of vaccination. The obverse has a cow and the necessary implements – the hypodermic and the tube with the vaccine. It is a lovely animal, accurately drawn, but the engraving by Depaulis lacks the charm of the Illyrian medal and the daring imagination of Denon's *La Vaccine*.

There are a number of other instances in which Denon, his artists and engravers, used and improved upon images from antiquity. Galle's crocodile chained to a palm tree, celebrating the conquest of Upper Egypt, is clearly superior to the crude bronze of Augustus from a mint in Gaul where troops that had been in Egypt were stationed.

The disastrous English attack on Antwerp in 1809, while Napoleon was in Vienna, inspired a splendid interpretation of the Olympian Zeus, as *Jupiter Stator*, the god who stopped the flight of the Romans from the Sabines. The artist knew his Livy and the application – Napoleon remaining unmoved at Schoenbrunn during the English attack while Jupiter crushed his enemies in the north – hits the

VACCINATIONS AT PARIS (1814), *EX INSPIRATO SALUS*. For the Paris Municipalities. A cow, source of the vaccine, with the equipment to deliver it. (Depaulis; Br. 1550), AR, 32mm.

CONQUEST OF UPPER EGYPT (1798). Crocodile chained to a palm tree copies a bronze *as* of Augustus from Gaul. Though dated 1798, the medal was not struck until 1806. (Galle; H. 896), 32mm.

BRONZE *AS* OF AUGUSTUS. The crocodile chained to a palm tree celebrates Augustus' victory over Antony and Cleopatra in 30BC. From the Namausus mint in Gaul, where some of the troops from Egypt were stationed.

JUPITER STATOR (1809). When the English attacked Antwerp in 1809, Napoleon was not alarmed and stayed in Vienna at Schoenbrunn, as the legend on the medal explains. *JUPITER STATOR* refers to a story of the Roman historian Livy who tells how Jupiter stopped an enemy attack, presumably as he caused the failure of the English attack on Antwerp. Napoleon's real confidence was in the swamps in the region of Antwerp, which spread disease among the English troops. The statue of Jupiter is a copy of Phidias' 60-foot high statue of Zeus at Olympia. (Domard; Br. 870)

NAPOLEON'S MEDALS: *'Victory to the Arts'*

THE CAPTURE OF VIENNA – A captive maiden weeping beside a trophy of Austrian arms laments the capture of Vienna. The captive maiden and trophy scene is a common ancient motif. Struck in Milan by Manfredini. (Br. 444)

mark. Domard's engraving of the 'father of gods and men' is worthy of Phidias who created the original.

The French clearly enjoyed the discomfiture visited by Jupiter on the hapless British Army while Napoleon stayed insouciantly at Schoenbrunn. *Le Moniteur* translated page after page from the English papers, first of details of the disaster and then of the investigation into the reasons for it while reporting casually from Vienna that 'Yesterday there was a grand parade at Schoenbrunn, His Majesty reviewed the regiment from Nassau and a part of his French and Italian Guard.'[32]

While praising Denon and the *Monnaie des Médailles* at Paris, one must say that Manfredini's workshop at Milan turned out medallions of comparable quality. What ancient weeping captive maiden figure can match the beauty of Manfredini's *VINDOBONA CAPTA*?

'VICTORY TO THE ARTS'

Most of the stolen art was returned in 1815 and the French artist wept, as we see him in a contemporary engraving,[33] when the Laocoon and the Apollo Belevedere in the background begin their homeward journey. The Italian art was lost to France, but a more authentic 'victory for the arts' remained. The medals themselves are artistic triumphs in creativity and technique and propaganda. No other hero of ancient or modern times has been as well served by his artists and engravers. In that sense, Napoleon's medallions are, indeed, the embodement of the legend 'Aux Arts La Victoire'.

'THE FRENCH ARTIST WEEPS AT THE FORTUNES OF WAR' as the Laocoon and the Apollo Belvedere begin their return journey to Rome in 1815. (Saunier, Conquêtes Artistiques, Pl. XII)

NAPOLEON'S MEDALS: *'Victory to the Arts'*

Notes

1. Letter to Napoleon (AN) 11, 27 July 1803. The first medal struck under Denon's Directorship of the Medal Mint. Other medals had been struck sporadically at the Paris Mint through the period of the Revolution and in the early years of the Consulate, also at Milan, and elsewhere.
2. AN 11.
3. *Le Moniteur*, 3 October 1803.
4. *Le Moniteur*, 5 March 1797.
5. Paul Wescher, 'Vivant Denon and the Musée Napoléon', *Apollo*, September 1964, pp.178–186.
6. *Lettres sur le préjudice qu'occasionnerait à la science le déplacement des monuments de l'art de l'Italie.* Saunier, p.45.
7. Published in *Le Moniteur,* 3 October 1796. Saunier, pp.51–54.
8. Hennin 811, p.568, refers to a notice in *Le Moniteur,* of 17 April 1798.
9. Charles Saunier, *Les Conquêtes Artistiques de la Révolution et de l'Empire*, Paris, Librairie Renouard, 1902. Pl. 4, p.37.
10. E. and J. de Goncourt, *Histoire de la Société Française pendant le Directoire.* Saunier, pp.36–37.
11. 26 July 1798.
12. *Le Moniteur's* enthusiastic and detailed description of the two-day festival and parade through Paris is very similar to the description in Plutarch's *Aemilius Paulus* of that general's three-day triumphal parade with wagons carrying statues, pictures and spoil.
13. Pl. LXI. Marcelle Brunet and Tamara Préaud, *Sèvres, Des origins à nos jours*, Fribourg (Switzerland), 1978.
14. Trans. by Edward Edwards, *The Napoleonic Medals*. London: Henry, Hering, & Paul, 1837, p.16. Edwards' book is a translation of the first half of the Empire section of George-Julian Fellmann, *Tresor de numismatic et de glyptique*, Paris, 1836.
15. As part of Denon's *médailles restituées*. In a letter of 11 January 1811, Denon explains his project of taking up each year neglected subjects: 'I take care each year to take up subjects previous to when I took over direction in order to complete as far a possible the medallic history of the Emperor.' National Archives 02 853, in Antony Griffiths, 'The Design and Production of Napoleon's *Histoire Métallique*' *The Medal*, 16 (1990), p.27.
16. Edwards, p.59.
17. Pierre-Francois-Leonard Fontaine, *Journal, 1799–1853*, I, pp.212–214. (2 vols., Paris: Ecole Nationale Superieure des Beaux-arts, 1987.)
18. Fontaine, *Journal* I, entry for 11 September, p.215.
19. Marie Louise Biver, *Le Paris de Napoléon*. Paris: Librarie Plon, 1963, pp.181–85.
20. In a book, *De l'Art de voir dans les Beaux-Arts.* Saunier, pp.55–56.
21. Nov. 26, 1808. Letter no. 14510.

22 AN 14.
23 L. de Lanzac de Labourie, *Paris sous Napoléon – Spectacles et Musées*. Paris: Librairie Plon, 1913, p.280.
24 AN 17.
25 *Le Moniteur*, April 26, 1803.
26 January 17, 1805.
27 On a medal dated 1804, but actually struck in 1809 as part of Denon's *médailles restituées* series.
28 Denon, *Corresp.* 783.
29 *Trésor* 5.4; Bramsen, no. 400.
30 Judith Nowinski, *Baron Dominique Vivant Denon (1745–1825)*, Farleigh Dickinson Univ. Press, 1970, p.59.
31 National Archives 022853, From Antony Griffiths, *The Medal*, 16 (1990), pp.28–29.
32 *Le Moniteur*, Oct. 13, 1809.
33 Saunier, *Conquêtes Artistique*, Pl. XII.

II

Napoleon and his Engravers

LANDING OF LOUIS XVIII AT CALAIS (1814). Andrieu's portrait of Louis XVIII, celebrating the King's arrival in France at his First Restoration. (Andrieu; Br. 1406)

The creative use of the symbols from classical antiquity – the movement beyond traditional barren allegory – was one reason for the success of the Napoleonic series of medals. A second was the 'hero' himself, a larger than life figure for whom the classical imagery, the imperial costume, the heroic trappings of Hercules, even the deification as Mars or Jupiter, were admirably suited. Napoleon was convincing in that role as no other historical figure of that or any other modern era. When the Bourbons returned to France in 1814 it fell to the artists to place Louis XVIII, also, in the heroic tradition. However, as Mark Jones remarks,

> The restoration, by robbing French medallists of the subject matter for medals in the heroic classical mode, deprived their style of its *raison d'être*. The features of Louis XVIII … defeated even Andrieu's attempts to endow them with classical nobility…[1]

The suitability of classical apparel for the image of Napoleon is apparent when the artist descends to the mere military. Chaudet's bronze statue of Napoleon as a Roman emperor atop the Vendôme Column, with mantle and laurel crown, was melted down in 1815, the metal used for an equestrian statue of Henry IV (1793), set up in 1817. The replacement by Louis Philippe on 28 July 1833 was totally inadequate – a dumpy figure, cast from sixteen pieces of cannon found in the arsenal at Metz, and described thus: 'The Emperor is represented with a telescope in his hand, and in the

NAPOLEON AND HIS ENGRAVERS

RESTORATION OF THE STATUE OF NAPOLEON (1833). Louis Philippe restored the statue of Napoleon to the Column of the Grand Army in 1833. Military dress replaced Chaudet's classical figure – a reduction to mere realism. Napoleon III returned it to the classical style in 1863 with a statue in imitation of Chaudet. (Montagny; Br. 1906), 23mm.

hat, military frock, sword, great-coat, and boots which he wore on the day of the battle of Austerlitz.'

The military costume leeched away the aura of the hero. Napoleon III's restoration in 1863 was a replica of Chaudet's statue – an appropriate return to the classical dress that suited the hero so well.

Another factor in the success of the series was the presence in Paris of a talented group of artists and engravers who knew how to use the classical themes. What was not generally understood until recent research in the archives revealed it, was that the artists as well as the engravers contributed substantially to the quality of the medals and that the artist-designers were recruited from the best painters, sculptors and architects of the day.[2] Vivant Denon, by virtue of his position as director of the Medal Mint, the Museum, the Sèvres porcelain factory, and Napoleon's unofficial artistic advisor for all of his public works, could choose whomever he wished.

NATIONAL ASSEMBLY – ABANDONMENT OF PRIVILEGES (4 August 1789). The deputies of the three orders take an oath to abandon their privileges and throw down their titles at the foot of the altar inscribed *A LA PATRIE*. A medal was voted in memory of the occasion. (N. Gatteux; H. 59), 64mm.

SIEGE OF THE BASTILLE (14 July 1789). Andrieu's first medal in which the confusion of soldiers, citizens, and their arms, all enveloped in a cloud of smoke, is remarkably detailed. (H. 23), 86mm.

NAPOLEON AND HIS ENGRAVERS

ARRIVAL OF THE KING IN PARIS (6 October 1789). The people bring the Royal Family back to Paris. Andrieu in a second medal skilfully details the confusion and the variety of the scene. (Andrieu; H. 62), lead 77mm.

PARIS COMMUNE – ATTACK ON THE TUILERIES (10 August 1792). Liberty holding a pike with a liberty cap tramples the symbols of royalty and hurls a thunderbolt. The storming of the Tuileries marked the end of the monarchy. (Duvivier; H. 363)

It was Vivant Denon's appointment as Director of Museums on 19 November 1802 and of the *Monnaie des Médailles* in September 1803 that was decisive for the success of the *Histoire métallique*. This is not to say that no beautiful medals had been produced before Denon took charge. Notably there were two by Andrieu in 1789 at the very beginning of his illustrious career: 'The Siege of the Bastille' and 'Return of the King to Paris'. Nicolas Gatteaux produced the 'Abandonment of Privileges' and 'The Constitution of the Year III'. Benjamin Duvivier struck 'The Attack on the Tuileries' and the splendid medal commemorating the arrival of the Italian treasures in Paris (H. 811). There were many other medals of various sizes, but it was Denon who brought order and purpose into the series and standardised it at 40mm. More than just his administrative skill, it was the Director's personal attention to detail in the design of many of the medals that was decisive. The signature on each of them – '*Denon direxit*' – was well earned.

31

NAPOLEON'S MEDALS: *'Victory to the Arts'*

▲ **COUNCIL OF THE ANCIENTS – CONSTITUTION OF THE YEAR III** (1795). (N. Gatteau; H. 789)

▲▶ **LAST FAREWELL OF LOUIS XVI** (20 January 1793). The guillotine for the next day is visible through the window. An English view of the French Revolution. (C.H. Kuchler), 48mm.

Meanwhile, the English were watching. Two poignant medals deal with the end of the monarchy. 'The Last Farewell of Louis XVI, with the guillotine visible out the window', and 'Marie Antoinette in a cart on the way to execution'.

Only a superficial viewing of Napoleon's medallions is necessary to prove that they were done by a most talented group of engravers. And as previously pointed out, there was an important role played by the artist-designers in their creation.[3] The artists' payment was usually 1/25th to 1/35th of that for the engravers, but we should not assume from that discrepancy that the artists were workshop hacks. Among them were the prominent painters, sculptors, and architects of the day. These included the painters, Pierre Bergeret, the famous Pierre Paul Prudhon, and Alexandre-Everiste Fragonard, son of the well-known painter Jean Honoure Fragonard. There was also Chaudet the sculptor, Lepere the architect, and Meynier the painter and the designer of sculptures for the Carrousel Arch.

At the very beginning of Napoleon's medal design stands the painter, Andrea Appiani, whom Napoleon discovered at Milan during the first Italian Campaign and commissioned to draw four of the series known as 'The Five Battles' for the engraver Lavy. Appiani included versions of these medals in the fresco frieze he painted in the ballroom of the *Palazzo Reale* in Milan.[4] His importance is suggested by the fact that he signed a later medal, for the victory at Marengo in 1800 (Br. 42), something the medal designer seldom dared to do. Appiani continued to draw over the years for the splendid series engraved by Manfredini and his workshop in Milan.

The sculptor Antoine-Denis Chaudet – who did the much praised statue of Napoleon for the Legislative chamber and the statue of Napoleon as a Roman emperor atop the Column of the *Place Vendôme* – designed about a dozen of the medals. Pierre Bergeret, at the beginning of a long and illustrious career, was given the task by Denon of designing the frieze for the Column of the *Place Vendôme*. Bergeret designed several medals for Denon, including the creative vision of Napoleon smiting the Giants while riding Jupiter's eagle (Br. 538) for the Battle of Jena. Griffith believes that Denon suited the character of the design desired to the particular professional expertise of the artist.[5]

Among engravers, Bertrand Andrieu of Bordeaux produced more medals for Napoleon than any other. Andrieu came to Paris to study with the great engraver, Nicolas Gatteux. His abilities soon became apparent with the production of two large *clichés* (85 and 78mm), masterpieces of incidental detail in two critical moments at the beginning of the Revolution, the storming of the Bastille and return of King Louis to Paris (H. 62).

Andrieu's work of the Napoleonic era include the beautiful *La Vaccine* (Br. 400), his Peace Maiden for the Peace of Luneville (Br. 107), the Cupid and Hymen for the marriage of Jérôme Napoleon (Br. 662), for which Prudhon drew the design, and finally the extraordinary 68mm image of Napoleon raising his son above the baptistery in Notre Dame – the baptism of the King of Rome (Br. 1125).

Andre Galle learned the art of engraving at a Lyons button factory and got his start at Paris by engraving a much-praised head of the revolutionary leader Mirabeau. He received the Decennial Prize for his portrait of Napoleon on a 68mm medal celebrating the Coronation festivities (Br. 358), for the Battle of Friedland (Br. 632), and several other medals.

Rambert Dumarest was honoured for his view of the Peace of Amiens in 1802, Napoleon offering an olive branch to Britannia (Br. 195). Dumarest's premature death in 1806 was a great loss to engraving and was occasion for a long eulogy in *Le Moniteur*.[6] Nicolas Brenet, who began his career during the Consulate, was one of the most prolific of Napoleon's medallists, producing over 50 pieces and continuing his distinguished career far into the subsequent era of French history.

The career of Jean-Pierre Droz is most interesting in political and artistic versatility. A Swiss who came to Paris before the Revolution, he struck several coins and medals for the French monarchy and invented an improved coin press. Unappreciated by the French government, he went to England in about 1790, where he worked for Matthew Bolton in Birmingham. In 1799 he returned to France, and was appointed Keeper of the Coins and Medals by the Directory. Napoleon appointed him Keeper of the Mint Museum in 1804, a position that he held until 1814. He is noted as the inventor of several more refinements to the minting process.[7] Droz was also one of Denon's best engravers. Returning to England at the end of the war, he contributed several medals to Mudie's National series.[8]

Andrieu, Brenet, Dumarest, Galle, Gayrard, Jeuffroy, and Droz were probably the best of Napoleon's engravers at the Paris *Monnaie des Médailles*. To this list

NAPOLEON'S MEDALS: *Victory to the Arts*

must be added Luigi Manfredini, mint engraver at the Milan Academy of Arts for many years. His contributions to the Napoleon medals rival the most beautiful of the Paris Mint series.

Bonaparte was most fortunate in his artistic director, Vivant Denon, since the Emperor-to-be understood art primarily as propaganda and had little interest in or understanding of artistic theory or aesthetics. Chaptal, Minister of the Interior under the Consulate, reported that Napoleon never stopped before any of the works in his museum without demanding coldly, 'What is that about?'[9]

Born a member of the lesser nobility in 1747,[10] Vivant Denon had a somewhat erratic career as courtier to Louis XV, diplomat, and artist before Napoleon invited him on his expedition to Egypt. In Egypt Denon braved enemy fire to make his sketches. This exhibition of courage in the service of art impressed Napoleon, as did Denon's broad experience and knowledge of the European art scene gained during years in the French embassy at Naples. Jacques Louis David badly wanted the position of Director of Fine Arts, but Napoleon wisely saw that David, though the greater artist, lacked Denon's breadth and depth of knowledge and the courtier's talents of personal diplomacy.

VIVANT DENON AT HIS DESK. Vivant Denon (1747–1825) was Napoleon's Director of Museums from 1802 and of the Medal Mint from 1803. He often himself selected the designs for Napoleon's medals. (Saunier, *Conquêtes Artistiques*, Pl. VIII)

There is some evidence of collaboration between Napoleon and Denon on specific medals, but usually the Emperor left the choice to his talented Director, reserving the final approval to himself. When an ancient design from a coin or cameo was suitable, Denon had only to resort to his own extensive collection assembled in large part during his diplomatic career in Naples. Two old engravings show Denon at work.[11]

The minting press used was the double crank hand-operated screw type, called a 'fly press', similar to that invented by Nicolas Briot early in the seventeenth century. Significant improvements were made by Jean-Pierre Droz. The beautiful miniature medal of 1813 by Brenet (2-12; Br. 1303), and the drawing from Forrer,[12] illustrate the operation.

The usual procedure in the Napoleonic era was for an officially commissioned artist to do a drawing from which the engraver would engrave the die. A wax model was sometimes made. The die was hardened for use in the production of

NAPOLEON AND HIS ENGRAVERS

thousands of medallions in gold, silver, and bronze. A 'hub' was usually made for additional dies when the original wore out. '*Clichés*' – trial pieces for medals produced in limited numbers – often in lead or pewter, are also found frequently.

There is a poignant parallel to the achievement of Denon and his engravers at the Paris *Monnaie des Médailles*. The *Commission des Inscriptions et Médailles*, a division of the *Classe d'Histoire et de Littérature Ancienne* of the French Academy, laboured for seven and a half years, July 1806 to February 1814, to create the *Histoire Métallique de l'Empereur*, a series of medals to glorify the Emperor and his achievement.

'DENON AT WORK IN THE MIDST OF THE OBJECTS OF ART.' An old engraving. (Saunier, *Conquêtes Artistiques*, Pl. V)

35

NAPOLEON'S MEDALS: *Victory to the Arts*

MINTING PRESS (1813). Struck in honour of Marie Louise's (fictitious) visit to the Medal Mint (Brenet; Br. 1303). The press was developed by Nicolas Briot in the seventeenth century and improved by J.P. Droz. The diagram shows operation of the press by hand. (L. Forrer, ed. *Biographical Dictionary of Medallists*, New York, 1970, Volume I. p.164.)

The result was three volumes of 156 drawings of medals commemorating the great events of Napoleon's career from his return from Egypt in 1799 to 1808.[13] The drawings were beautifully bound in blue Morocco leather to be presented to the Emperor. The drawings of medals were intended eventually to be struck. A fourth volume was planned but never completed.

The members of the *Commission* were a distinguished group of a half dozen or so scholars and artists, most of whom had significant careers outside the Commission. Ennio Visconti had held important administrative posts related to the arts in Rome, had been a consul of the short-lived Roman Republic and had written important books on ancient art. He was for many years Conservator of the ancient collection of the Louvre under Denon.

Quartremere de Quincy was known for his works on Jupiter Olympus, the Parthenon, and studies on Raphael and Michelangelo. Of the two artists who did the drawings, Antoine Chaudet was the sculptor who did the statue placed in the legislative chamber and made the bronze of Napoleon placed on top of the Column of the *Place Vendôme*. Baron Lamot executed the chariot and the two Victories beside it, teamed with the bronze horses from Venice on top of the Carrousel Arch and also the imperial statue that Napoleon denied a place in the chariot.

The minutes of the *Commission* which met weekly are filled with earnest discussions by the five Commissioners about subjects and designs, about the language to be used – Latin was decided upon – and the Calendar, Gregorian or Julian. That question was never resolved. The designs had then to be approved by the *Classe d'Histoire et de Littérature Ancienne*, which sometimes rejected a design, or insisted on its revision.

The *Commission* continued its work faithfully until February 1814. The minutes of their meetings betray not the slightest echo of the Empire falling apart around them during Napoleon's last desperate campaign. They simply cease on 18 February 1814 with the barren administrative note; 'Meeting adjourned at 3 o'clock.'

On the fall of Napoleon the three volumes with their 156 drawings were in the apartment library of Baron Dacier, Perpetual Secretary of the *Commission*, where he was accustomed to work. There they remained until his death in 1833. The work was never presented to the Emperor and only one of the medals was ever struck, that for the Battle of Jena. (Br. 537).

There is one curious incident recorded in the minutes of the *Commission*, which suggests the possibilities if there had been any cooperation at all between the two artistic centres. The Mayors of Paris requested the design for a medal to commemorate their visit to Vienna, to Schoenbrunn, where Napoleon was staying after the brilliant campaign of Austerlitz, to thank him for a gift of enemy cannon and standards. The representation of this scene was to be accompanied by an allegory on the reverse.

Visconti responded for the *Commission* with a brilliant, brief description of a design for a medal (Br. 453; 68mm), which was then drawn by Lamot and struck at the Paris Mint. Though among the largest and most beautiful of the Napoleonic series, the *Commission* decided it could not fit it into its narrowly conceived plan for the *Histoire métallique* and proposed a different design for its own use.

One must wonder why only one of this elaborate series, created by several of the best scholars in the country and drawn by the talented Chaudet and Lamot, was ever produced. The weight of the Academy bureaucracy is hardly the whole explanation. More likely is the fact that Denon controlled the machinery of production and had no interest in promoting a rival to his own series. Like scholars everywhere, the learned members of that fraternity took pleasure in doing their scholarly best at the task in hand, taking no interest in the political challenge necessary to bring their work to fruition. We should regret more this waste of scholarly and artistic talent if we did not have the extraordinary series of medals struck under Denon's direction at the Paris *Monnaie des Médailles*. In 1851, Dacier's son, Edme, presented the three volumes of drawings to the *Bibliothèque Nationale* where they languished until finally published by Ernest Babelon in 1912.

A perspective on the financial situation of the Medal Mint and its engravers is provided by J.J. Guiffrey's researches in the National Archives.[14] It is clear that the income from sale of medals came nowhere near paying the bill. The operation was heavily subsidized by the government. Nor did the premier engravers of the Medal Mint become rich. Two of Napoleon's best and most often employed engravers, Galle, in 1811, and Brenet, in 1812, wrote to Perne, Controller of the Mint, pleading desperately for commissions. Galle insists he is willing to do almost anything.[15]

An old engraving[16] gives an inspired impression of the multi-talented Director of the *Monnaie des Médailles* (page 35). He sits 'at work in the midst of the objects of art', a chaos of books, statues, paintings, bas-reliefs, public monuments, and a minting press – bringing order out of all of it! And drawing from all of these elements he created the most brilliant era of medal art in history.

Notes

1 *The Art of the Medal,* London: British Museum Publications, 1979, p.102.
2 Antony Griffiths, 'The Design and Production of Napoleon's *Histoire Métallique,*' *The Medal* 16, 1990.
3 Most important in this respect has been the research of Antony Griffiths in the Paris National Archives, set forth in three articles in *The Medal* 16–18, 1990–91.

4 Griffith, *The Medal* 16, (1990), p.16. Destroyed during the Second World War, p.25, n. 3.
5 *The Medal* 16 (1900), p.18.
6 *Le Moniteur*, 17 October 1806, notes: 'With these traits you recognise an artist whose character is as noble as his talent is worthy of estimation.'
7 J. J. Guiffrey, 'La Monnaie des Médailles d'après les documents inédit des Archives Nationales,' *Revue Numismatique*, 3rd series, vol. IV (1886), pp.90, 97.
8 Jean-Pierre Droz, in L. Forrer, ed., *Biographical Dictionary of Medallists*, Vol. I, pp.429–442.
9 Chaptal, *Mémoires*, p.270, cited in Lelièvre, p.93.
10 For biographies of Denon see Judith Nowinski, *Baron Dominique Vivant Denon*, Rutherford, Madison, Teaneck, 1970; Musee du Louvre, *Dominique-Vivant Denon, L'oeil de Napoléon*. Paris, 1999.
11 Saunier, *Conquêtes Artistique*, Plates V and VIII.
12 L. Forrer, ed., *Biographical Dictionary of Medallists*, Vol. I, p.164.
13 Ernest Babelon, *Les médailles Historiques du règne de Napoléon le Grande, Empereur et Roi*. New York: New York Numismatic Society; Paris: Ernest Leroux, Editeur, 1912. See this volume for all details about the work of the *Commission*.
14 J.J. Guiffrey, 'La Monnais des Médailles d'après les documents indédits del Archives Nationales,' *Revue Numismatique*, 3rd Series, iv (1886), pp.86–100.
15 Guiffrey, pp.94–96.
16 Saunier, *Conquêtes Artistiques*, Pl. V.

III

Napoleon – God and Hero

NAPOLEON AS HERCULES (1806). *Napoleon le Grand* wearing the lion skin of Hercules. The hero's club is in the field, Napoleon's star after the date. The thunderbolt really belongs to Jupiter. The reverse lists victories of the Prussian campaign of 1806. (By 'B.M'; Br. 554), 52mm.

From ancient times conquerors have enlisted the support of gods and heroes to justify and magnify their deeds. Where the imagination of the conqueror fails there have always been flatterers to fill the need. Napoleon was no exception. An excerpt from a conversation with Gourgaud on St Helena shows succinctly what we know from his whole life, that Napoleon did not shrink before such flattery. 'In China the sovereign is worshipped as a god' he said, 'That, I think is how it ought to be.'[1] The medallion, with its tradition of allegorical reference to antiquity and myth, was available to Napoleon's flatterers – his artists and medallists.

POST HERCULEOS LABOURES REPORTATAS UNO ANNO CXI VICTORIAS, boasts the reverse of the *ITALICUS* medal of 1797 (H. 812), placing Napoleon in the tradition of the quintessential ancient hero Hercules, the most appropriate incarnation of Bonaparte. Hercules, who once roamed the world performing his labours for the benefit of mankind, now served France and Bonaparte. Napoleon himself was Hercules on a portrait medal of 1806 showing him with the attributes of the hero, lion skin and club, with Jupiter's thunderbolt thrown in for good measure. The reverse is a list of the principal battles and conquests of the year 1806 inscribed within a laurel wreath.

The medal for the victory at Millesimo and Dego (April, 1796) in the First Italian Campaign shows Hercules slaying the many-headed Hydra of Lerna, appropriate for the general who had to fight several Austrian armies at once. The hero attacks the beast with a club in his right hand and with his left holds one of its heads. His right foot is on its tail. Under the left

NAPOLEON – GOD AND HERO

foot is the torch with which he burned the heads of the monster as they regenerated.

In 1804 Hercules, in preparation for the invasion of England, ties up the Nemean Lion, also the British lion (Br. 320 on p.103). 'In the year 12 2000 boats have been built' boasts the legend. In this first of Hercules' twelve labours, according to the ancient story, the hero initially attacked the beast with sword and club, but failed since the lion's skin was impervious to wood and metal. That approach having failed, Hercules strangled it with his bare hands, then skinned the beast with its own claws. The lion skin was part of Hercules' raiment from that moment on. Ancient representations most frequently show Hercules strangling the lion as does the Roman *denarius* from 80BC, and at first glance the Paeonian *tetradrachm*. Closer inspection, however, shows that the hero's right arm is missing. Other examples of the same coin show him clearly attacking the lion with a sword, an earlier phase of the struggle. On the three tiny *diobols* from Tarentum (overleaf) several stages in the fight may be seen.

On the French medal, the engraver, Droz, has gone beyond all variations of the ancient scene. The hero is in the act of tying up the lion, never part of the legend.

The final victory is assumed in another medal of the year 1804 showing Hercules wrestling Antaeus, who, because he gained his strength from the earth is held in the air by the hero. The victory is affirmed in the over-optimistic legend, in the exergue, 'Struck in London in 1804'.

Obviously the medal was never struck. It exists only as a trial piece, but the medal that eventually went into circulation was indeed struck in London, or at least in England, by Matthew Bolton, whose principal mint was in Birmingham. The British somehow got hold of the design after the war and made a copy to mock Bonaparte's failure.

Other labours of the hero were reinvented by Napoleon's artists. Lavy's medal of 1800, which the artist Appiani dared to sign along with the engraver, shows Napoleon as Hercules raising and restoring the Cisalpine Republic in a medal that celebrates the victory at Marengo in June of that year. A withered bush beside which the maiden reclines suggests her previous condition, but now the sun rises on a new day with Napoleon's star at its centre. The hero's club and lion skin lie on the ground behind him. An inscription boasts, 'Twelve highly fortified cities were forced to surrender on the same day.' The Cisalpine Republic was Napoleon's 1797 creation from three north Italian republics, Milan, Bologna, and

HERCULES SLAYS THE HYDRA – BATTLES OF MILLESIMO AND DEGO (1796). Hercules slays the many-headed Hydra; Bonaparte defeated several Austrian armies in the First Italian Campaign. (Appiani; Lavy; H. 733)

HERCULES STRANGLING THE NEMEAN LION. Roman silver *denarius* (80BC). This was the first of Hercules' twelve labours. As the lion's skin was impervious to wood or metal, the hero had to strangle it.

HERACLES FIGHTING THE NEMEAN LION. Three Tarentine *diobols* show various stages in the struggle (fourth–third century BC).

HERACLES FIGHTING THE NEMEAN LION. Paeonian *tetradrachm* (fourth century BC). Right arm off the flan probably held a sword.

NAPOLEON – GOD AND HERO

Modena, after the First Italian Campaign. It had to be restored after the Austrian re-conquest of northern Italy during Napoleon's sojourn in Egypt. The Second Italian Campaign brought northern Italy and the Cisalpine Republic back under French control. The decisive French victory is inscribed by Victory on a shield: *HOSTIBUS PROPE MARENGUM FUSIS*.

Hercules continued to perform for Napoleon throughout his career. In a medal of 1805 Napoleon/Hercules receives from two captive women representing their cities the keys of Vienna and Pressburg, the fruits of his victory over Austria in that year.

The victory at Wagram in July 1809 that ended the Second Austrian Campaign was memorialised by a medal showing Hercules vanquishing a giant, from whom he rescues Victory (Br. 860). According to the ancient Greek myth of the battle between the gods and the giants, the gods, in desperate straits, called in Hercules because only a mortal could vanquish the giants. This myth is reflected in several other medals. The scene is repeated in a medal celebrating the French victory of Borodino before Moscow in 1812. On a large 55mm medal by Droz, Hercules slays the giants while the French eagle hovers above.[2]

Napoleon's son, born in March 1811, also becomes part of the Hercules legend. He is portrayed as the infant Hercules in his cradle, strangling snakes sent by a jealous Hera.[3] Hercules was the son of Zeus by one of his many mistresses, hence Hera's jealousy. The medal copies a favourite scene of ancient artists, a typical example of which may be seen on a fourth-century BC silver coin of the South Italian Greek city of Croton. The conceit is not too bold for a baby with a name like Napoleon Francis Joseph Charles, and the title 'King of Rome'.

◄ 'STRUCK IN LONDON, 1804.' Hercules tames Antaeus, holding him to prevent his touching the earth from which he derives his strength. Designed to be struck after a successful invasion. Later English copy of a medal never produced in France. (Jeuffroy; Br. 2188)

▲ CISALPINE REPUBLIC RESTORED (1800). Napoleon/Hercules raises the Cisalpine Republic, restored after the Battle of Marengo in June 1800. Napoleon's star appears at the centre of the rising sun. (Signed by Appiani; Lavy; Br. 42), 53mm.

NAPOLEON'S MEDALS: *'Victory to the Arts'*

◀ **CAPTURE OF VIENNA AND PRESSBURG** (1805). Captive maidens surrender their cities to Napoleon in the role of Hercules. (Chaudet; Andrieu; Br. 443)

◀ **BATTLE OF WAGRAM** (1809). The Battle of Gods and Giants. Hercules wins the battle for the Gods, vanquishing a giant and rescuing Victory who holds a quill-pen and a crown. Defeat of Austria, in the final Battle of the Second Austrian Campaign. (Lafitte-Fragonard; Galle; Br. 860)

▼ **BATTLE OF MOSCOW** (1812). French victory before Moscow, 7 September 1812. Hercules again slays the giants, while the French eagle hovers above. (Droz; Br. 1162)

We also find a British Hercules, paired with a splendid head of Britannia with a lion on her helmet (Br. 1441). He stands repeating a favourite ancient theme, 'the repose of Hercules' and trampling a French standard. May we be permitted to see this medal, dated 1814, as Wellington, after years of successful campaigning, resting before Waterloo? The engraver is none other than the master, J. Droz, now working for the British, who produced two of the French Hercules medals.

44

NAPOLEON – GOD AND HERO

◂◂ THE BABY HERCULES strangling snakes in his cradle. Silver *nomos* from Croton, Greek city in South Italy,. (370 BC).

◂ THE BABY HERCULES (1811). Napoleon's son, the King of Rome, as the infant Hercules strangling snakes in his cradle. (From Prince Essling's Auction Catalogue, 1927, Pl. XLI; Schmidt; Br. 1108)

◂ REPOSE OF HERCULES (1814). Celebrating the Peace of Paris. Hercules resting after his labours (a common ancient theme) and trampling a French standard. (Droz; Br. 1441)

The image of 'Mars the Peacebringer', the illusion that war is the best way to peace, has always come easy to the leaders of armies. It was prominent in the era of the Roman Barracks Emperors in the third century AD, when emperors appeared and disappeared as fast as their armies made and unmade them. Coins of two rulers of this period, Gallienus and Claudius Gothicus, illustrate the type, Mars carrying both an olive branch and a spear, with the legend MARTI PACIFERO ('Mars the Peacebearer').

Napoleon and his engravers shared this vision. Bonaparte himself appears a number of times as the god of war who brings peace. On a medal of 1797, Napoleon as Mars receives the surrender of Mantua (2 February 1797), which

45

NAPOLEON'S MEDALS: *'Victory to the Arts'*

ended the First Italian Campaign. A maiden wearing a civic crown hands him the keys of the city. In the background is an aqueduct and a part of the city fortifications.

On Dumarest's medal of 1802, Napoleon/Mars cradles victory in his left arm while offering an olive branch to a recumbent Britannia leaning on an unhappy looking British lion. The implied boast of the medal is near the truth. The reference is to the Peace of Amiens. A number of British statesmen shared the lion's discomfort, in spite of a medal featuring the 'Marquis Cornwallis, Plenipotentiary

'MARS THE PEACEBEARER.' Coins of the third century AD. Emperors Gallienus and Claudius Gothicus. Mars bears a spear and olive branch. *MARTI PACIFERO* is the legend.

SURRENDER OF MANTUA (1797). Napoleon as Mars receives the surrender of the city of Mantua in February 1797, ending the First Italian Campaign. (Appiani; Lavy; H. 785)

NAPOLEON – GOD AND HERO

at Amiens', and declaring this a 'Definitive Treaty' (Br. 204). The peace signed in March 1802 was clearly unfavourable to England and could not last.

The final distillation of the myth of 'Mars the Peacebringer' is found in the association of Napoleon with Diogenes, the founder of the Cynic school of philosophy. According to the ancient story, Diogenes searched in vain for an honest man all his life. Napoleon's artists insist that in Napoleon the philosopher has found him. For the industrial exhibit of 1806 a bronze clock was crafted showing Diogenes with his lantern pointing to a standing figure of Napoleon who is being crowned by Victory. On the front of the base Fame and History record the Emperor's heroic deeds.[4] The clock was a great success with visitors to the exhibition.

In the same year the Medal Mint produced a trial piece with a similar scene (Essling, 1145). Diogenes with his lantern points to a portrait of Napoleon saying, *JE CHERCOIS UN HOMME*. In the exergue appears, *JE L'AI TROUVE*. As if in proof of the philosopher's conclusion, a column behind him records twelve of

PEACE OF AMIENS (1802). Napoleon as Mars, holding Victory on one arm, extends an olive branch to a suppliant Britannia, leaning heavily on an unhappy British lion. French view of the Peace of Amiens of 1802. (Dumarest; Br. 195), 48mm.

47

NAPOLEON'S MEDALS: *'Victory to the Arts'*

NAPOLEON AND DIOGENES (1807). Diogenes ends his search for an honest man by blowing out his lantern. 'I have found him!' he exclaims, pointing at a portrait of Napoleon. A column behind Diogenes, listing Napoleon's victories, is presumably the proof of Diogenes' discovery. (Dr. Julius' Auction Catalogue, Munich, 1932, Pl. 25, No. 1820; Br. 679). A clock, on the same theme, was a popular item at the Industrial Exhibition of 1806. (Napoleon, 'Wonders', Memphis International Cultural Series, 1993, No. 109)

Napoleon's military victories, from Montenotte, in the First Italian Campaign, to his defeat of the Prussians at Jena in 1806. In the next year on another trial piece the theme is updated.[5] Diogenes is shown blowing out his lantern, his search concluded, and exclaiming, *JE L'AI TROUVE*. The column records only Napoleon's most recent victories, from Ulm to Friedland. Neither piece was ever struck for circulation.

The ultimate apotheosis is Napoleon as Jupiter, Bergeret's creative vision, engraved by Galle. Napoleon rides Jupiter's eagle among the clouds, smiting the Titans who would ascend to heaven at the Battle of Gods and Giants (Br. 538). This is Bergeret's view of the Battle of Jena (14 October 1806). Not an absurd image, if you discount the affront to Greek mythology, for the battle was an overwhelming victory that 'completely calmed that warlike madness that had seized the Prussian brain'.[6]

Notes

1. Elizabeth Wormeley Latimer, trans. and ed., *Talks of Napoleon at St Helena with General Baron Gourgaud*. Chicago, 1903, p.102.
2. Certainly by Droz, but probably a later strike.
3. Prince Essling's Auction Catalogue, Pl. XLV.
4. Bernard Chevallier, *Napoleon*. Memphis, 1993. Memphis Exhibition Catalogue, plate 109.
5. Dr. Julius' Auction Catalogue, Munich, 1932, Pl. 25, No. 1820.
6. Fifth Bulletin of the Grand Army, *Le Moniteur*, 26 October 1806.

IV

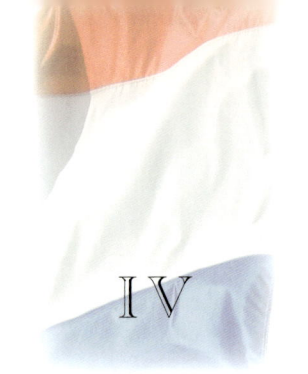

The Conquest of Nature

Nature itself must awake in astonishment at the achievements of the hero, Bonaparte, or bend to serve him. No surprise that Napoleon's engravers would use the symbols of nature to glorify Napoleon as the ancients had done for their rulers.

Heaven and Earth

In ancient iconography Victories usually performed rather prosaic tasks, driving chariots, flying with wreaths to crown a hero, erecting trophies, trumpeting a military triumph. In Napoleon's world, Victories also become a catalyst for his mastery of nature. Even when doing the expected they sometimes performed more than their usual task, as in Duvivier's medal for Campoformio (H. 811),

OCCUPATION OF HANOVER (1803). Victory rides furiously into Hanover, the 'land of fine horses'; this was Napoleon's response to the English breach of the Treaty of Amiens. (Chaudet; Jeuffroy; Br. 271)

THE CONQUEST OF NATURE

where the Victory who crowns Napoleon also brings the Apollo Belvedere to Paris. The lovely Victory who symbolises the triumph at Wagram in 1809 wields a thunderbolt, not a usual part of her equipment. She may do even more startling things – ride a cannon for a chariot over the Alps, remembering Napoleon's swift crossing of the mountains into Italy before Marengo in 1800, or ride a horse furiously into Hanover, signifying Bonaparte's swift conquest of that country in response to England's breach of the Treaty of Amiens in 1802 – more particularly because Hanover was noted for her fine horses.

The treaty of agreement for the British withdrawal was careful to specify that all the horses of the Hanoverian Army be turned over to the French, both cavalry and artillery horses.[1] After the takeover, *Le Moniteur* reported the army in a most satisfactory situation, having taken possession of 4,000 horses; 'these horses are very beautiful!'[2] Hanover's horses were still the focus when the British Army re-entered the country in 1814. The reverse of an English medal celebrating the re-conquest (Br. 1489) showed Britannia feeding two horses.

BATTLE OF WAGRAM (1809). Victory hurls a thunderbolt in celebration of Napoleon's defeat of the Austrians. Final battle of the Austrian Campaign. The thunderbolt is apt: at Wagram, Napoleon's artillery came of age. As his artillery commander, *Général de Division* Jean-Ambroise Baston commented, 'I have never heard such a cannonade and it lasted 45 hours.' (Manfredini; Br. 862)

CROSSING THE ST BERNARD (1800). Victory rides a cannon, cradled in a hollowed-out log, a device Napoleon used in crossing the Alps. Napoleon's rapid march led to victory at Marengo, the decisive battle of the Second Italian Campaign. (Fragonard; Dubois; Br. 37; not struck until 1809. Part of Denon's *médailles restitutées*.)

NAPOLEON'S MEDALS: *Victory to the Arts*

BATTLE OF AUSTERLITZ (1805). Charlemagne (or Napoleon?) enthroned on a thunderbolt. His decisive victory over Russia and Austria, 2 December 1805. Two days after the battle, the Austrian Emperor Francis sought an armistice and Tsar Alexander I retreated back to Russia. (Chaudet; Jaley; Br. 445)

PEACE OF LUNEVILLE (1801). The sun shines on the Continent of Europe but a cloud obscures England. (Droz; Br. 106), 54mm.

The thunderbolt itself became a throne for the Emperor Napoleon,[3] appropriate for the brilliant victory of Austerlitz since before the battle he had promised his soldiers, 'This campaign must be finished by a thunderclap which shall confound the pride of our enemies.'

Sun and clouds were used to dramatise the French view of the political situation after the Peace of Luneville in 1801. Over a map of Europe, the sun shines on the continent while clouds obscure England, an accurate assessment of the meaning of the Peace for the British.

River gods and water nymphs were an obvious symbol to dramatise the geography of military conquest. The Nile, with the Pyramids on the reverse, naturally symbolises the conquest of Lower Egypt. The Tiber, on a medal celebrating the union of France and Italy in 1809 watches the French eagle return to the Capitol, carrying a thunderbolt. The Roman wolf suckles a single child, not the legendary twins. One wonders why – the reason is not as clear in this instance as it is for the medal celebrating the birth of the King of Rome in 1811 (Br. 1094, p.176).

THE CONQUEST OF NATURE

These images are passive, like their originals – nothing exciting or creative here. Other river gods are used more imaginatively. Perhaps when there was no ancient model the artist was freer to imagine the dramatic event, in most cases the arrival of the French Army. The Vistula, on Brenet's beautiful medal, is a lovely nymph who reveals 'an attitude expressive of grief at the sight of the French eagle planted on her shores'.[4]

Some deities react more animatedly to the arrival of the French. The Tagliamento starts up in surprise as Bonaparte appears in the distance with his army, crossing the river on the way to Trieste (Italian Campaign, spring of 1797). The Raab, leaning on his urn, seems unmoved as the army of Prince Eugene passes him by in the Austrian War of 1809, but behind him a peasant flees to the mountains (Br. 854).

Two Russian river gods are startled by the appearance of the French Army in 1812. The Borysthenes, sitting on his throne, turns with a start, and the Volga flees

CONQUEST OF LOWER EGYPT (1798). The Nile (copy of a statue in the Vatican); the Pyramids are on the reverse. (Not struck until 1810; Brenet; H. 850)

REUNION OF FRANCE AND ITALY (1809). The god of the Tiber (copied from a statue in the Louvre) watches the French eagle (also Jupiter's bird) return to Jupiter's temple on the Capitol – *AQUILA REDUX*. (Lafitte; Andrieu; Br. 848)

FRENCH ARMY ON THE VISTULA (1807). A nymph, spirit of the river, hangs her head, to reveal 'an attitude expressive of grief at the sight of the French eagle on her shores'. (Chaudet; Brenet; Br. 620)

THE CONQUEST OF NATURE

PASSAGE OF THE TAGLIAMENTO (1797) and taking of Trieste. The river god starts up at the approach of the French Army. Earliest of a number of medals in which rivers react to Bonaparte's victories. (Appiani; Lavy; H. 787)

FRENCH EAGLES BEYOND THE RAAB (1809). The god of the river reclines on his urn. Battle won by Prince Eugene on 14 June 1809 while Napoleon – having re-crossed the Danube after his defeat at Essling on 22 May – was proceeding toward the final victory at Wagram on 6 July. (Fragonard; Dubois; Br. 854)

in terror at the sight of the French standards, while a sturgeon, 'a fish common in those waters'[5] jumps from the river.

The angry god of the Danube provides an excuse for one of Napoleon's rare defeats. In May 1809, Napoleon threw an army across the rain-swollen river at Essling with the help of pontoon bridges, from one bank to the Island of Lobau in the centre of the river and from there to the far bank. The army narrowly escaped but with heavy losses, when the angry Danube, *PONTEM INDIGNATUS*, broke up the bridge from the French side to the island.

A medal shows the god in the act of destruction. On the broken bridge are a cannon and two French standards. A successful crossing downstream six weeks later allowed Napoleon to balance the defeat at Essling with a victory at Wagram.

55

BATTLE OF ESSLING

(1809). The god of the Danube, angry at Napoleon's bridge, reacts violently, destroying it – *DANUBIUS PONTEM INDIGNATUS*. Napoleon was forced to withdraw. (Fragonard; Brenet; Br 859)

CROSSING THE DANUBE

(1809). French troops crossing the Danube with Victory flying above. The Archduke Charles inflicted on Napoleon his first clear defeat at the Battle of Essling (20–22 May). The French excuse was that the angry Danube had broken up Napoleon's bridge of boats. Napoleon recovered quickly however, and six weeks later engineered a skilful crossing of the river downstream. This led to the decisive victory at Wagram and the Treaty of Schoenbrunn. (Fragonard; Brenet; Br. 859)

THE CONQUEST OF NATURE

The reverse of the same medal shows the army marching victoriously across the new bridge.

Boreas, the North Wind, and the brutal Russian winter of 1812 can be blamed for the disastrous French retreat from Russia in that year. Boreas with his bag of winds chases a helmeted warrior from the land, wrapped in a skin for warmth. Dead horses, an abandoned wagon and cannon may be seen behind. In a letter of 18 November Napoleon complained bitterly of the loss of horses, not only for cavalry but also for transport.

> Frost, and bitter cold, of sixteen degrees have killed almost all our horses – 30,000 of them. We have been forced to burn more than 300 pieces of artillery, and an immense number of ammunition-chests …[6]

A feature of Napoleon's arrogance was that he considered himself master of the earth in a very literal sense and of all those of its inhabitants who came within his control. Only he knew what was best for them and for the country in terms of government, education and religion. Whatever harm it may have done, from this supreme self-confidence came some most useful projects and some very valuable reforms.

Roads, mountain passes and canals were obvious projects for the conquest of nature that could be celebrated in medals. The Simplon Pass, a better route

RETREAT FROM RUSSIA (1812). A French warrior flees before Boreas with his bag of winds. The field is strewn with the debris of battle – horses and wagons. The loss of horses was a severe blow to Napoleon's ability to wage war in the next phase of the struggle. (Galle; Br. 1168)

FRENCH EAGLE ON THE BORYSTHENES (1812). The god of the river, seated on his throne, turns in alarm at the presence of the French eagle behind him. (Brandt: Br. 1158)

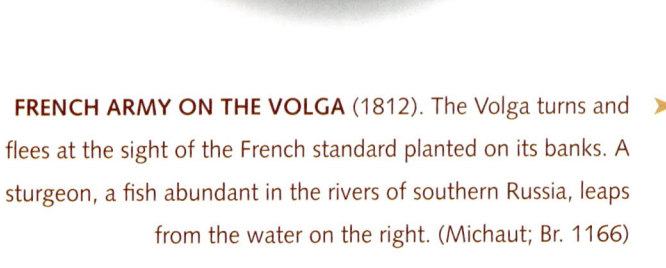

FRENCH ARMY ON THE VOLGA (1812). The Volga turns and flees at the sight of the French standard planted on its banks. A sturgeon, a fish abundant in the rivers of southern Russia, leaps from the water on the right. (Michaut; Br. 1166)

SIMPLON PASS (1807). An old man seated among mountains. Of enormous size, he dwarfs the figures of soldiers proceeding among a winding road who in the end are climbing the body of the giant himself. Under construction from 1800 to 1807, some 40 miles long by 26 feet in width, near the Great St Bernard. Napoleon called the Alps – made more passable by the Simplon – 'one of the monuments of nature which art has conquered'. (*Le Moniteur*, 29 August 1807). English copy by Durand (after 1834) of original by Brenet. (Durand; Br. 689)

58

THE CONQUEST OF NATURE

through the Alps, was begun in 1800 and completed in 1807. Napoleon in his 'State of the Empire' speech of 29 August 1807, described the Simplon as one of 'the monuments of art' and the Alps which the Simplon had made more passable as one of the 'monuments of nature that art has conquered'.[7] The medal struck to commemorate this achievement is worthy of it.[8] An old man of enormous size, seated among the mountains, dwarfs the groups of travellers that proceed along the mountain path which becomes the limbs of the giant himself. Daru, predictably, offered niggling criticism of the design – the giant was not noble enough and the path of the travellers was wrong, objections easily disposed of by Denon.[9]

The alternative to the transalpine route from France to Italy, difficult in the winter snows, was the road along the coast. In this case, travellers – and armies – had to contend with steep cliffs. Here again Napoleon demonstrated his mastery over nature with a road from Nice to Rome, begun in 1807. For a medal to celebrate this achievement Denon had a model ready at hand, a *denarius* of Trajan, advertising the *via Traiana*, a road running south from Rome. The coin showed Vibilia, Goddess of the Ways, reclining with her wheel. The medal by Raymond Gayrard (Br. 690) has improved the scene to make clear this conquest of nature. The goddess, seated in a cleft chiseled from the cliff, has one foot on the road, the other in the sea, and her hand on a mountain. It is interesting to find a medal for Napoleon's sister, Elisa, Duchess of Piombino and Lucca, using a similar scene to represent her construction of a road from Pisa to Lucca (Br. 774).

THE VIA TRAIANA

Vibilia, Goddess of the Ways, reclining with a wheel, commemorating construction of the *Via Traina*, the road south from Rome to Brundisium which replaced the Appian Way. *Denarius* of the Emperor Trajan (AD 98–117).

ROAD FROM NICE TO ROME (1807). Vibilia, Goddess of the Ways, seated on the road begun in 1807, built along the coast from Nice to Rome to avoid the mountain roads to France, impassable in winter. Copied from the denarius of Trajan, but the design has been improved, making the engineering achievement clear. The goddess' hand is on a mountain, one foot on the road and the other in the sea. (Not struck until 1813. Lafitte; Gayrard; Br. 690)

THE OURCQ CANAL (1809). The City of Paris is bathed by two nymphs whose jars of water are named *SEQUANA* (the Seine) and *URCA* (Ourcq). There is a ship in the background. (Fragonard; Andrieu; Br. 868)

THE CONQUEST OF NATURE

A medal celebrating the completion of the Ourcq Canal to the Seine shows the City of Paris with a ship in the background, bathed by two nymphs, whose jars read *SEQUANA* (the Seine) and *URCA* (Ourcq). The canal, begun in September 1802, was completed and opened with great ceremony on 15 August 1809, much improving the water supply for the city of Paris and shortening navigation time on the Seine.[10]

Medicine

Napoleon's smallpox vaccination programme, so beautifully endorsed by the Venus de Medici (Br. 400, p.18), must certainly be included in Napoleon's 'Conquest of Nature'. Vaccination was introduced into France in 1800, the first experiment being the vaccination of 30 Parisian children on 1 June with vaccine sent from London. On 29 March 1801 was announced the formation of a Central Committee for Vaccination, followed by intense efforts to educate the public and facilitate distribution. In April 1804 a society of well known scientists was formed for the propagation of the new medical procedure. The original heroic effort, however, was that of the Central Committee for Vaccination. The pages of the early months of *Le Moniteur* for 1801 are full of the efforts of the Committee to educate the public, to organise distribution, to fight hoarding and charlatanism, and to deal with the after-effects of vaccination. At least three books were published on the vaccine in the first months of 1801.

The two medals citing vaccination as an achievement appear a ten-year afterthought. Although Denon's medal was first proposed in 1806, it was not struck until 1812. The silver medal for the Paris Municipalities (Br. 1550, p.22) did not appear until 1814. Surely the heroic efforts of the Central Committee working with the Paris Mayors and the Prefect of the Department of the Seine was honoured before 1814, but that recognition does not appear before then on the medals.

Aesculapius, the physician god, appears again on a medal of 1805, in honour of the establishment of a School of Medicine in Paris. He stands with his hand on his serpent-entwined staff. Beside him is his son Telesphorus.

THE SCHOOL OF MEDICINE (1805). The physician god, Aesculapius, and his son Telesphorus. The medal commemorates the founding of a School of Medicine at Paris. Evidence of Napoleon's interest in medical science. (Joannin; Br. 467)

NAPOLEON'S MEDALS: *'Victory to the Arts'*

Education

Naturally, under Napoleon's ultimate control were all forms of learning. A medal by Andrieu celebrates his organisation of public instruction in 1802. A Roman youth, wearing the *bulla* which signified that he had not yet reached the age of fourteen, is seated on a stool, reading a scroll. There is a palm before him and a box of scrolls at his feet. Above his head is a star of destiny, shared with Bonaparte, the promise of a bright future.

The reorganisation of the schools was ordered in the spring of 1802[11] but Napoleon's ideas on education were formed and expressed before this, and of course continued to develop after they were put into place. That the symbol of this educational system should be studious Roman youth was appropriate for the eventual system. Latin and ancient history were an important part of secondary education and even to a lesser degree for primary students (those under twelve), as appears in Napoleon's instructions to Chaptal, Minister of the Interior

ORGANISATION OF PUBLIC INSTRUCTION (1802). A Roman youth seated on a stool, reading a scroll. A palm is before him and there is a box of scrolls at his feet. Above his head is the star of Destiny. A law of 1 May 1802 organised public instruction, from primary schools to the *lycees*, paid for by the public treasury. (Andrieu; Br. 214)

THE CONQUEST OF NATURE

in June 1801. Secondary school pupils were to be divided into those destined for a civil or military career. Those destined for a civil career would receive a classical education, 'ancient languages, principally Latin, and the full course of rhetoric and philosophy. They would also be taught the first volume in the course of mathematics.' Those headed for a military career would go through all four volumes of mathematics, adding required skills such as astronomy, drawing and fortification.[12]

The organisation and support of the primary schools was left to the communes, with the result that they were often neglected. Napoleon's chief interest was in the secondary schools and in particular the elite government-supported *lycées*.

Napoleon's views on the education of girls appear most cogently in a note on the establishment of the girls' school at Ecouen written on 15 May 1807.[13] A medal of 1810, (Br. 980) titled *ORPHELINES DE LA LEGION D'HONNEUR*, illustrates his opinion on female education expressed in this letter. A girl is seated with her back against a tomb, with downcast eyes, a book on her lap and a

ORPHELINES DE LA LEGION D'HONNEUR

(1810). A girl seated before a tomb with a book on her knees and a workbasket in front of her. Several schools were founded for the education of daughters, sisters, nieces, cousins of members of the Legion of Honour. The girls were to be kept busy with handiwork. Religion was encouraged, but not the study of philosophy.

workbasket at her side. We know something about the school itself because Josephine's daughter Hortense became its patroness, and from the writings of the Directress Madame Campan. The school is described as a main building, a remodelled chateau, 'surrounded by five orphanages for small children of heroes who had died in battle'.[14] The school was for *Orphelines,* daughters, wives and sisters of deceased veterans.

Napoleon's views on the education of girls can be interpreted from the medallion. The girl wears a frock with long sleeves: 'But of course they [the frocks] must have long sleeves.' She holds a book, perhaps one a little too thick for Napoleon's requirements. The girls were to be taught to read, but with careful restrictions. They should be taught 'writing, arithmetic, and the principles of their language, so that they know how to spell. They should learn a little geography and history, but be careful that they see no Latin or any foreign language ...' The older girls might learn a little botany, natural history, and physics 'to avoid crass ignorance or foolish superstition, but these studies must be concerned with facts, without reasonings which deal directly or indirectly with first causes'.

The workbasket beside the girl is the key symbol and expression of Napoleon's chief purpose expressed in the letter.

> But in general they all must be kept occupied during three quarters of the year with manual work. They must learn how to make stockings, shirts, and embroidery and all kinds of women's work ... I would like a girl who leaves Ecouen who finds herself at the head of a small household, to be able to make frocks, mend her husband's clothes, make clothes for her babies, procure sweets for her family such as a provincial household can afford, nurse her husband and children when they are sick.

The downcast eyes of the girl on the medallion may mean only that she is mourning for her deceased soldier father – she is seated in front of a tomb – but her demeanour does agree with Napoleon's insistence that Ecouen produce 'not women of charm, but women of virtue. Their attractiveness must be from morals and from the heart, not because they are witty or amusing.'

Napoleon insisted on mass every day in his letter to Lacepede, Grand Chancellor of the Legion of Honour,[15] more strict in this regard than Madame Campan, directress of the establishment, who thought Sunday and Thursday would be sufficient.[16] The reasons for Napoleon's insistence on the strict teaching of religion are transparent. For religion was 'the surest safeguard for wives and husbands. What we want is believers and not thinkers.'

In September 1807, Napoleon appointed Madame Campan mistress of Ecouen, who in her school at St Germain had the charge of educating several of the Bonaparte clan: Pauline, Caroline, and her favourite, Hortense. Madame Campan was fully in accord with Napoleon's purpose, to turn out women of virtue, good wives for France's heroes. She wrote how she explained that purpose in detail

THE CONQUEST OF NATURE

after lunch to the Emperor Alexander of Russia when he visited Ecouen in 1814.[17] The Emperor was impressed, according to Mme Campan, saying that there were many parallels between the organisation of Ecouen and those that the Queen, his mother, had established in her own similar house in St Petersburg.

The Arts

The arts and artistic expression were, of course, under Napoleon's control. What may be seen on the medals is primarily the display of his architectural enterprise in Paris, notably the Carrousel Arch (Br. 557) and the Column of the P*lace Vendôme* (Br. 463). In this case, in contrast to the ill effect of his control of the press, literature, and religion, the result was praiseworthy; Napoleon left his stamp on everything.

An engraving of Madam Campan, from her autobiography. Napoleon appointed her director of Ecouen in September 1807. (Depaulis; Br. 980)

NAPOLEON'S MEDALS: *Victory to the Arts*

FRENCH SCHOOL OF FINE ARTS IN ROME (1812), 're-established and augmented by Napoleon in 1803'. Between two branches of laurel forming a crown in the ancient style is a head of Minerva, around which are arranged the attributes of the fine arts. This beautiful medal, with a splendid portrait of Napoleon on the reverse, was Gatteaux's tribute to the French school. Though dated 1812, the medal was not issued until 1814. (E. Gatteaux; Br. 1178), 58mm.

The reorganisation of the School of Fine Arts in Rome was praised in a splendid medal by one who benefited from it, Edouard Gatteaux. Edouard had studied with his father, Nicolas Gatteaux, one of the great medallists of the late eighteenth century and produced his first medal, 'The Capitulation of Mantua' in 1808 (H. 782, p.76). In 1809, his medal 'Mars Following Victory' won him the *Prix de Rome*.[18] He studied in Rome until 1814. His tribute to the school is a head of Minerva, surrounded by the attributes of the fine arts; on the reverse is a unique portrait of Napoleon enthroned (Br. 1162, p.158). He returned to Paris in 1814, on the threshold of a long and distinguished career as an engraver.[19]

Religion

When it came to religion, Napoleon preferred to deal with recognised institutions to which he might grant certain privileges, but through which he might maintain control. Prudence was required to achieve the proper balance between freedom and control. This is the message of the medal for the Concordat of 1802 with the

THE CONQUEST OF NATURE

REESTABLISHMENT OF RELIGION (1802). France holds in one hand a mirror in which a serpent looks at itself, symbolising Prudence, with the other hand she raises a sad Religion, seated on the ruins of a church. Near Religion are a book and a cross. In the centre is a shield with a thunderbolt, mounted on a *fasces*, the Roman magistrate's symbol of authority. A cock on the shield is the emblem of vigilance (or of France). The church of Notre Dame is in the background. (Andrieu; Br. 213), 50mm.

Roman Catholic Church (Br. 213), which restored the Church to its place as the favoured religion in France but maintained strict controls. France is pictured as Prudence, identified by the snake looking at itself in a mirror which she holds in her left hand. With her right hand France raises a disconsolate Religion seated on a ruined church. Notre Dame is in the background, the symbol of stability in the religious chaos created by the Revolution.

The negotiation of the Concordat, signed on 8 April 1802 and celebrated on Easter Sunday, was an act of the highest wisdom by Bonaparte. He understood that France must be a Catholic country and over many months came to an agreement more or less satisfactory to both sides. The latent symbolism of the medal, however, a sword and shield on a *fasces*, the Roman magistrate's symbol of authority, indicates the real locus of power. A cock on the shield may stand for France, but could also be a symbol for watchfulness.

The Emperor's control may be seen in the provision that Bishops were to be nominated by the First Consul and clergy chosen by the bishops and that salaries of the clergy were to be paid by the state, to which the clergy were to swear allegiance. Bonaparte's close attention to the behaviour of the clergy is apparent

NAPOLEON'S MEDALS: *'Victory to the Arts'*

in many of his letters. Two are succinct and instructive. To M. Portalis, on 19 September, 1805: 'Inform M. Robert, a priest at Bourges, of my displeasure at the extremely bad sermon he preached on 15 August.'[20] And more extraordinary, to M. Bigot de Preameneu, Minister of Cults. 'Inform me why the Archbishop of Aix has ordered a Novena for the illness of Queen Louise, and why the public should be told to pray for anyone without the permission of the Government.'[21] That this letter was omitted by the editors of Napoleon III's official edition is no surprise.

The original version of the Concordat would have been a workable agreement but the 'Organic Articles' tacked on by Bonaparte, exploiting an ambiguous clause in the Concordat, clearly put the state in control and excluded Rome and the Pope's representatives from any effective action in France.

Napoleon's relation to the Jewish community is of considerable interest and appears on one medal, 'The Grand Sanhedrin'.[22] The occasion is a meeting of the Grand Sanhedrin, formed of leaders of the Jewish communities from all over the Empire, summoned by Napoleon in May 1806 to consider their privileges

THE GRAND SANHEDRIN (1806). Napoleon standing with the two tablets of the Law in his hands. Before him is a Rabbi in the form of Michaelangelo's Moses. Commentators say that this symbolises the Jews of the Grand Sanhedrin, called by Napoleon in September 1806, presenting their formulation of their own laws and customs to Napoleon. It looks, however, as if Napoleon (as God?) is giving the tablets of the Law to the Jews, which is really closer to the truth. (Engraved by Brenet but not struck until after 1815 in England; Br. 527)

68

and responsibilities to the French State. Napoleon shared the common mistrust of the Jews but prudence directed, as in the case of the Catholic Church, that it was better to have an organised body, granted some privileges, which he might control. The assembly did not actually meet, however, until February 1807 and presented its final report in March of that year.

On the medal, Napoleon in elaborate imperial costume stands holding two tablets, presumably the Law. Before him a figure, copied after Michaelangelo's Moses, kneels with upraised arm. The *Trésor*, followed by Bramsen and Essling, see a Jewish rabbi presenting the tablets of the law to Napoleon. A first glance at the medal suggests Napoleon as God, giving the Law to Moses. That interpretation, not beyond the arrogance of Bonaparte, is probably close to the truth, for the document presented to the Grand Sanhedrin[23] was a series of 'suggestions' incorporating Napoleon's intentions, which the Assembly had no choice but to adopt. The most important provisions were restrictions on money lending and the insistence on the payment of taxes and service in the army.

There is an interesting exchange of letters[24] found in the National Archives between Denon and Daru, to whom Napoleon at this busy time had delegated the approval of the medals to be struck at the Medal Mint. The thinly veiled hostility between the two civil servants is easily discerned beneath the superficially civil dialogue. Denon accepted without protest Napoleon's sometimes irrational objections to his medal designs, but one can detect a certain resentment at correction by Daru, one whose judgment he must have regarded as inferior to his own. Daru objected to the depiction of the Battle of Essling.

> It seems to me that the Battle of Essling is not represented so happily. It requires a commentary, which is inconvenient. The subject is complicated; the separation of the two parts of the army and the second crossing are very difficult to express.

Denon replied

> With regard to the one for the Battle of Essling, may I have the honour of pointing out to you that I had an accident to express here, that it was necessary to present the river which causes it by breaking the bridge, which divided the army, which is expressed by the two standards that the reverse shows; the remedy that repaired this misfortune is a great example at the same time of confidence and subordination.

Denon continued with an insight into his philosophy of medal design.

> In general medals have a hieroglyphic manner of explaining themselves, and if they often are an aid to history, history itself, often, quite naturally sometimes comes to the aid of the medals. That of the Battle of Essling presents at the same time two important facts; it looks fine and offers no political inconvenience, so permit me to retain it.

Notes

1. *Le Moniteur,* 8 July 1803.
2. *Le Moniteur,* 14 August 1803.
3. If indeed it is Napoleon. Some scholars have suggested Charlemagne.
4. Edward Edwards, *The Napoleon Medals.* London: Henry Hering & Paul, 1837, p.66.
5. *Trésor* 54.11.
6. Lloyd, No. 303.
7. *Le Moniteur,* 29 August 1807.
8. The medal displayed is an English copy by Durand with slight differences from the original by Brenet (Br. 688).
9. Griffiths, *The Medal* 16, (1990) pp.28–29.
10. *Trésor* 33.3.
11. Proposed to the Legislature, 20 April 1802, (*Le Moniteur,* 22 April 1802).
12. Corresp. 5602.
13. Corresp. 12585. Letter to A.M. Lacepede, Grand Chancellor of the Legion of Honour on 22 October, 1807.
14. Constance Wright, *Daughter to Napoleon,* New York, 1961, p.203. Books by and about Mme Campan include *Journal anecdotique de Mme Campan, ou Souvenirs Recuillis dan ses Entretiens, Par M. Maigne, Médecin des Hôpitaux de Mantes,* Paris: Baudoin Frères Libraries, 1824. Gabrielle Reval, *Madame Campan, Assistant de Napoléon,* Les Vies Authentiques, 1931. Violette M. Montagu, *The Celebrated Madam Campan,* Philadelphia: J.B. Lippincotte Company, 1914.
15. Corresp.13284. 22 October 1807.
16. Montagu, *The Celebrated Madame Campan,* p.299.
17. *Journal anecdotique de Mme Campan,* p.46–50.
18. *Le Moniteur,* 8 October 1809.
19. L. Forrer, *Biographical Dictionary of Medallists,* II, 206.
20. Corresp. 9243. 19 September 1805.
21. Design by Denon, but struck in England after 1815. Lecestre, *Lettres Inédites.* I, 417. 3 March 1809.
22. Engraved by Brenet, according to the *Trésor* (13.15) from a design by Denon, but struck in England after 1815.
23. Corresp. 10686.
24. Reprinted in Antony Griffiths, 'The Design and Production of Napoleon's *Histoire Métallique*', *The Medal,* 16 (1990), 27–30.

V

First Italian Campaign

'Napoleon's whole life was a retrospect of history' wrote Ann Mudie Scargill in the introduction to one of the first commentaries on the medals. 'His imagination was excited by the examples of the Caesars and Alexanders.'[1] The medals from the First Italian Campaign of 1796 to the end of Napoleon's career bear out this judgment.

The boast on the reverse of the *ITALICUS* medal – a private issue struck to mark the end of the Italian Campaign[2] – shows this most clearly. The inscription takes one's breath away: *ALEXAND. BUONAPARTE: POST HERCULEOS LABORES REPORTATAS UNO ANNO CXI VICTORIAS. ITALIAE LIBERATORI. EUROPAE PACIFICATORI.* Bonaparte as Alexander, performing the labours of Hercules, in one year liberated Italy, pacified Europe, and reported one hundred and eleven victories!

ALEXAND. BUONAPARTE POST HERCULEOS LABORES (1797). Private issue of an Italian tobacco merchant at Strasbourg, Etienne-Bernard Mainoni, celebrating the Treaty of Campoformio on 17 October 1797, which ended the war. Probably he hoped to gain something from Napoleon – which he did! In 1802 he was appointed Director General of the Italian tobacco factories at Milan. Obverse on p.10. (H. 812, pewter)

NAPOLEON'S MEDALS: *Victory to the Arts*

For all of the exaggeration, Napoleon's First Italian Campaign was a remarkable achievement. Taking a rag-tag, dispirited and undersupplied army, he skilfully met and defeated in turn several Piedmontese and Austrian forces, winning Piedmont and northern Italy for France and driving the Austrians back into their homeland.

Bonaparte ordered his own series commemorating the Italian Campaign, at Milan (later known as 'The Five Battles') where he held court in the summer of 1797. Four of these were engraved by Lavy after drawings by the Italian painter, Appiani, who incorporated the same designs in a huge mural painted on a wall of the royal palace.[3] Bonaparte's portrait does not appear on any of the official issues, one supposes because such a device would have been viewed in Paris as too bold.

Other private admirers of Bonaparte knew no such restraint. One of the earliest of these private issues is a silvered bronze by Pierre Ferrier of Geneva (H. 767, p.147), celebrating the first victories in Italy. Bonaparte in uniformed bust is addressed as 'General in Chief of the Brave Army of Italy'. The reverse is Minerva seated on a trophy of arms, holding a branch of laurel and oak and leaning on a shield with the Roman *fasces*. The brave soldiers are enjoined to 'behold the fruit of your labours'. There were also private issues by the city of Lyons and in a number of German states, but in Austria one could be arrested for merely possessing a medal with Bonaparte's portrait.

The issue of Lyons by Jean Marie Chavanne (H. 816) to celebrate the Treaty of Campoformio, featured a young bust of Bonaparte with long hair addressed to the 'General in Chief of the Army of Italy' by the 'citizens and artisans of Lyon'. The reverse of the medal has peace holding an olive branch and a horn of abundance. In front of the goddess is an altar on which are two hands joined. The legend in the exergue says 'He does not fight except for peace and the rights of man.' The Lyonais, apparently, still thought of Bonaparte as one who fought for the 'rights of man'. Three years later Chavanne did another very similar medal (Br. 59) with Bonaparte's hair a little shorter.

The private issues not only featured Bonaparte's portrait but often included extravagant laudatory inscriptions; the *ITALICUS* medal discussed above is an excellent example. One medal (H. 762), probably produced in Germany, compares Bonaparte with Italy's ancient invaders. 'At his name, Rome still trembles … He effaces the glory of Hannibal and Brennus.'[4] Rome did indeed tremble at Bonaparte's name. The choicest Vatican treasures were ceded to France by the Treaty of Tolentino and later Napoleon bullied the Pope with impunity.

The first of 'the Five Battles' was a medal for the victories of Millesimo and Dego, 13 and 14 April 1796 (Br. 844, p.141), the decisive battles by which Napoleon liberated Piedmont and broke through to the Plain of the Po. The series might have begun with Bonaparte's very first victory a day earlier, on 12 April, when he routed the Austrians at Montenotte.

FIRST ITALIAN CAMPAIGN

The medal for Montenotte was struck sixteen years later as part of Denon's *médailles restituées*. Its vision is both historical and prophetic. Victory carrying unsheathed sword, palm, and crown, flies over a map of southern Europe with Italy at the centre. Flying eastward, 'she seems prophetically to direct her course towards those parts of the globe where Bonaparte was destined to carry the French arms triumphant.'[5]

The medal for the victory at Millesimo and Dego expresses his tactics in the whole campaign very well. Hercules slays the many-headed Hydra, attacking its heads one by one – as Napoleon did the armies of Austria.

The taking of the bridge at Lodi over the River Adda was the next spectacular action of the campaign, as the Austrians retreated eastward. The French Army, led by Generals Massena and Berthier, crossed the bridge under heavy fire. The medal by Salwick dramatises the event. This victory was not one of great strategic importance; the battle was only with Beaulieu's rear guard. But the bold action caught the imagination of the French people and ensured that Bonaparte would not be superseded. '*La patrie*' was 'grateful to the Army of Italy' as the reverse of the medal declares.

BATTLE OF MONTENOTTE (1796). Not struck until 1813. First of Napoleon's Italian victories. Victory flies eastward over a map of Italy. (Lafitte; Jeuffroy; H. 731)

NAPOLEON'S MEDALS: *Victory to the Arts*

BATTLE FOR THE BRIDGE AT LODI (10 May 1796). First Italian Campaign. Massena and Berthier lead the troops across the bridge under heavy fire. This action caught the imagination of the French and henceforth Bonaparte's removal was inconceivable. (J. Salwirck; H. 376)

The medal commemorating the Battles of Castiglione and Peschiera (5–6 August 1796) shows two nude warriors in heroic combat. Another, already fallen, lies on the ground. The apparent victor is about to give his adversary still standing a fatal blow.

The scene is the echo of countless similar ones from antiquity, but Hennin suggests a special meaning for this combat of a hero against two warriors, the defeat of the two Austrian armies of Italy and the Tyrol by a single French army. At Castiglione, Napoleon stopped the Austrian general Wurmser in his formidable attempt to retake the plain north of the Po, having previously frustrated the attempt

FIRST ITALIAN CAMPAIGN

of Quasdanovich, moving southward to unite with Wurmser at the southern end of Lake Garda. The Battles of Castiglione and its sequel at Peschiera were much more significant than the taking of the bridge at Lodi.

The surrender of the strategic city of Mantua on 2 February 1797 – which effectively ended the First Italian Campaign – was celebrated by two medals. On Appiani and Lavy's contemporary piece (H. 784) Mars (Bonaparte) receives the key to the city from a turreted lady, a personification of the city. On Edouard Gatteaux's first medal (H. 782) struck much later in 1808, Bonaparte (or Gatteaux) remembers Mantua by picturing Virgil, her most famous citizen, whose

CASTIGLIONE AND PESCHIERA (1796). One warrior fallen. Bonaparte defeated the Austrian general Wurmser in battles much more decisive if less celebrated than Lodi. (Appiani; Lavy; H. 744)

NAPOLEON'S MEDALS: *'Victory to the Arts'*

CAPITULATION OF MANTUA (1797). Wurmser, holding Mantua, surrendered on 2 February 1797, not 30 January as on the medal, ending the First Italian Campaign. This medal, the first of Edouard Gatteaux's successful pieces, remembers VIrgil, whose home city was Mantua. The reverse shows a mural crown and a swan, emblems of the city. (E. Gatteaux; H. 782), 35mm.

Aeneid immortalised Augustus. On the reverse is a mural crown and a swan, 'emblematic of the Bard's sweet verse' suggests Captain Laskey, who asserts that 'the conqueror of Italy was no less desirous of fame than Augustus: Virgil was in his recollection.' Laskey's further statement, that Napoleon ordered that the city's inhabitants 'should be indemnified for all the losses they had sustained by the war', must be qualified by the knowledge that Mantua, as most other cities taken by Bonaparte, was forced to surrender its best art treasures. Admiration for Virgil is not to be confused with respect for the city's art.[6]

Lavy's medal (H. 487) for the passage of the Tagliamento and the taking of Trieste (March and April, 1797), the first of the alarmed river god series, reflects Bonaparte's subsequent eastward thrust, which led to the Treaty of Campoformio in the autumn (17 October 1797), so humiliating for Austria, in which she lost most of northern Italy.

There is an interesting footnote to the *ITALICUS* medal (page 10), struck for the Treaty of Campoformio[7] – the discovery that it was issued by an Italian, Etienne-Bernard Mainoni, who in 1797 was in the tobacco business at Strasbourg. Mainoni also sponsored another medal, praising Bonaparte for the happy conclusion of the Treaty of Rastadt, 1 December 1797 (H. 880). Undoubtedly, Mainoni shared with many north Italian small businessmen the pleasure of seeing the Austrians run out of Italy, but there may be another motive behind this entrepreneur's expenditure. As mentioned earlier, In 1802 Mainoni was appointed Director General of tobacco manufacturing at Milan by Bonaparte's young Italian Republic, perhaps the goal he had in mind when he issued his medals.

Another of the medals struck in honour of that treaty, Benjamin Duvivier's issue for the National Institute (H. 811), of April 1798, with Victory crowning Bonaparte while holding manuscripts and the Apollo Belvedere, reflects also the Treaty of Tolentino (19 February 1797) with the Pope. The treasures secured by that treaty were already on their way and would arrive in Paris to great celebration in July 1798.

Bonaparte was not present at the celebration. At the head of the *Armée de l'Orient* he had landed in Egypt on 28 June.

Notes

1 Anne Mudie Scargill. See also Antony Griffiths, 'The end of Napoleon's *Histoire Métallique*', *The Medal 18* (1991), 35–49. Griffiths makes a good case from notations on a British Museum copy of Scargill's manuscript and from a comparison of the 1815 Medal Mint List that the introduction to the Mudie-Scargill manuscript is by James Mudie, publisher of the English National Series of medals and that the manuscript itself is a translation of an original by Denon.
2 Struck at Strasbourg, in pewter, for the Treaty of Campoformio by Etienne-Barnard Mainoni.
3 Destroyed in the Second World War.
4 Henin 819, p.574.
5 Scargill, p.2.
6 Laskey, pp.12–13.
7 Henin, No. 812–814, 880, pp.569–71, 615.

VI

Egypt

It is the Egyptian campaign that reveals Bonaparte as the 'New Alexander', the role claimed for him on the *ITALICUS* medal. His well-known conversation with his staff on the eve of Austerlitz is filled with Alexander imagery.[1]

> Had I taken possession of Acre [in 1799], I should have worn a turban; I should have put my army into wide trousers; I would no longer have exposed it except in the last extremity; I should have finished the war against the Turks with Arabs, Greeks and Armenians. Instead of a battle in Moravia, I should have won a battle on the Issus, created myself Emperor of the East, and returned to Paris by way of Constantinople.

Many historians regard the French Egyptian Campaign as a complete disaster. Napoleon himself, however, considered the 'time I spent in Egypt … the most beautiful of my life', for 'in Egypt I found myself freed from the obstacles of an irksome civilization. I was full of dreams and saw the means by which I could carry out all that I had dreamed.'

Even after the loss of Egypt, his letters reveal that Napoleon did not completely abandon his dream of conquering the East. In one way, even without that conquest, Napoleon's retrospective on Egypt was right. It was the dream that went beyond mere conquest that led to the real achievement of the Egyptian Campaign, Napoleon's determination to pursue scholarly research in that country. For that purpose he took with him an impressive team of 167 scholars. In Cairo he founded the Egyptian Institute, from which eventually emerged his most enduring monument, the *Description de l'Egypte*, published in ten folio volumes, on which the scholarly establishment worked for twenty years. One may add, of course, the discovery of the Rosetta Stone by one of Napoleon's soldiers, which, though it ended up in England as the spoils of war, provided the means of deciphering the Egyptian hieroglyphic script by the Frenchman Champollion. The real legacy of Napoleon's Egyptian Campaign was the birth of the discipline of Egyptology.

The Egyptian Campaign produced no immediate medallions except in England. Bonaparte was completely cut off from his European base. The English, on the other hand, had both the means and the incentive to produce a number of medals celebrating their victory.

EGYPT

It is surprising that even after Bonaparte's return to France and consolidation of his power as First Consul, and given his enthusiasm for what he regarded as the great achievement of his Egyptian conquests, the Egyptian medals were so long in coming. Of course the recovery of northern Italy was Bonaparte's first concern, and then there were the medals to celebrate the victory at Marengo.

This delay in producing the Egyptian medals was not due to lack of interest on Napoleon's part, however. On 6 September 1800 he wrote to Lucien, then Minister of the Interior, ordering six medals for the Egyptian campaign,[2] including one for the taking of Alexandria and the Battle of the Pyramids, one for the Battle of Aboukir, one for the conquest of Upper Egypt, the occupation of Qoseyr and the Cataracts, and one for the Battle of Heliopolis.

On 9 January 1801 Bonaparte wrote to Chaptal, who had replaced Lucien as Minister of the Interior, asking for a report on 'the medals which had been requested to perpetuate the memory of the principal military events of the war'.[3] The failure to meet Bonaparte's request may have been due to the inefficient management of the Medal Mint under the aged Cotte, or neglect by Lucien on his way out as Interior Minister.

The three Egyptian medals eventually produced were the Conquest of Upper Egypt (1806), the Conquest of Egypt (1808), and the Conquest of Lower Egypt (1810). Brenet's medal for the Conquest of Lower Egypt shows a finely detailed view of the Pyramids with the broken top of the Great Pyramid and the still intact casing on the top of the second. On the opposite face is a view of the Nile (H. 850), taken from a statue in the Vatican, for a time part of the collection in the *Musée Napoléon*.

The pyramid on Wyon's English medal (H. 857) is much more fanciful, and the medal's overloaded symbolism provided multiple justifications for the British celebration. An angel (or Victory) seated before the pyramid, with a skull, lion, harp and palm tree and wearing an Egyptian headdress, holds a picture of Nelson and a sword. An inscription, *VIRTUTE NIHIL OBSTAT & ARMIS* ('nothing resists his courage and his arms') lauds Nelson and his victory on 1 August 1798. The reverse reports and dates the celebration in England on 20 November 1798, three and a half months later. A ribbon around an anchor and shield contains the date and 'Praise to God', all under the radiant eye of God and the command Constantine read in the sky, *SUB HOC SIGNO VINCES*.

The medal for the conquest of Upper Egypt has the head of a Pharaoh, for years misidentified as Isis, and on the reverse a crocodile chained to a palm tree, borrowed from an *as* of Augustus (p.23) struck at Nemausus in Gaul, apparently for soldiers who had been with him in Egypt.

The medal for the conquest of all of Egypt shows Bonaparte in a chariot, drawn by a pair of richly caparisoned camels, passing between Cleopatra's Needle and Pompey's Pillar. The chariot is in Egyptian style and camels, Scargill notes, are 'animals which were more generally used than the cavalry horses of the French

VIRTUTE NIHIL OBSTAT & ARMIS Nelson's pyramid trumps Bonaparte's. He destroyed the French fleet at the Battle of the Nile on 1 August 1798, isolating Bonaparte in Egypt. A medal overloaded with symbolism. An angel (or Victory) seated before a pyramid, with skull, lion, harp, and palm tree, wearing an Egyptian headdress, holding a picture of Nelson and a sword. (Wyon; H. 857), W/M 39mm.

REVERSE OF H. 857. Celebration of Nelson's victory in England, 20 November 1798. The date is on a ribbon around an anchor and a shield that displays English arms and reads 'Praise be to God'. All is under the sign which Constantine read in the sky, *SUB HOC SIGNO VINCES*.

80

◀ **CONQUEST OF LOWER EGYPT – THE PYRAMIDS** (1798). Struck in 1810. Napoleon defeated the Mameluks at the Battle of the Pyramids. (Brenet; H. 850), 34mm.

▼ **CONQUEST OF UPPER EGYPT – A PHARAOH** (1798). For many years misidentified as Isis. Not struck until 1806. (H. 896), 34mm.

▲ **CONQUEST OF EGYPT** (1798). Bonaparte in a chariot drawn by two camels, passes between Cleopatra's Needle and Pompey's Pillar. Victory overhead is about to crown him. Bonaparte's conquest of all of Egypt was meaningless since Nelson's victory at the Battle of the Nile had isolated the French army, assuring its ultimate surrender. Not struck until 1808. (Fragonard; Brenet; H. 879)

▲ **BONAPARTE IN EGYPT – THE LEGEND** (1798). 'Soldiers: from the height of these Pyramids 40 centuries look down upon us': Napoleon's supposed words at the Battle of the Pyramids, 21 July 1798, although their verity is questionable. Struck 45 years later, 1843–45. (Bovy; Essling 769)

81

SYRIA SAVED; BONAPARTE REPULSED. The English lion protects the Syrian camel from a malicious French leopard. Sir Sydney Smith's force frustrates Bonaparte's attempt to take Acre. (Brenet; Mudie 7)

ADMIRAL SIR SYDNEY SMITH – WITH ALL HIS MEDALS. The opponent of whom Napoleon said, 'That man made me miss my destiny.' (Mills; Mudie 7)

army'[4] – but hardly to draw chariots! The rare frontal portrait of Bonaparte on the obverse (H. 879) is crowned by a wreath of Egyptian lotus rather than the usual laurel.

The most famous legend of the campaign – Napoleon haranguing his troops before the Battle of the Pyramids (21 July 1798) – does not appear on the original medals, but the scene is found on certain private uniface issues, designed, it is said, for snuff boxes.[5] Forty-five years after the event (1843–45), the scene was engraved by Antoine Bovy for the Medal Mint. Napoleon on horseback addresses the army and pointing to the Pyramids in the distance declares, 'Soldiers, from the top of these Pyramids 40 centuries look down upon us.' The circumstances leading up to the battle make it most unlikely that Napoleon ever said it.

Had Bonaparte taken Acre, would he have 'won a battle on the Issus', created himself 'emperor of the East, and returned to Paris by way of Constantinople'? Did Sydney Smith's lion opposing the French leopard save the Syrian camel, and the lands beyond from Bonaparte's aggression? This was Napoleon's impossible dream, as Alan Shom and others see it.[6]

The failure of the Egyptian Campaign was not evident to most Frenchmen on Bonaparte's 'fortunate' return on 9 October 1799. The French government of the Directory was in chaos and certain members were ready for a coup but needing 'a sword', which they hoped to find in the newly returned Bonaparte.

Notes

1 General Count de Ségur, *Memoirs of an Aide-de Camp of Napoleon 1800–1812*, revised by his grandson, trans. by H.A. Patchett-Martin. New York, 1895.
2 Corresp. 5087.
3 Corresp. 5264.
4 Scargill p.6.
5 Henin 848, 849.
6 Alan Schom, *Napoleon Bonaparte*, Harper Collins, New York, p.179.

VII

First Consul

MARENGO – KEYS OF CAPTURED CITIES (1800). Eleven keys of fortresses turned over to the French after Marengo. The obverse of this medal shows Victory riding a cannon-chariot over the St Bernard – Bonaparte's crossing into Italy before the battle. (Fragonard; Bubois; Br. 74)

Napoleon's squadron of small ships is seen on a medal arriving at Frejus (H. 921), having miraculously escaped the British fleet. Napoleon's lucky star is in the heavens. On the other side is the Roman god, *Bonus Eventus*, a statue of which is to be found in the Louvre.

Napoleon, on his return, found the French government of the Directory in chaos and certain members ready for a coup but needing a strong leader, which they hoped to find in Bonaparte, whom they mistakenly thought they could control. The result was the coup of 18 Brumaire (9 November 1799) from which emerged a Consulate of three members with Bonaparte firmly in control as First Consul, his superior authority confirmed by the Constitution of the Year 8 on 14 December 1799.

The sun rises from the sea dissipating the clouds; a medal proclaims the new era inaugurated by the events of 18 Brumaire (H. 923; Br. 57). But the reverse suggests another purpose, looking forward to the anniversary celebration of 14 July to be held at Nimes. It is to be in honour of the citizens of the Department of the Guard who had given their lives for the Republic.

Jean-Baptiste Dubois, who ordered the medal, added the name of Lucien Bonaparte, head of the Department of the Interior. As Prefect of the Department of the Guard he felt entitled to add his name also to those of the three Consuls.[1] The medal appears to have been struck at Lyons, the engraver being Mercie.

While Bonaparte was in Egypt, Northern Italy had been lost to France and the remaining French army in that country was in desperate straits. Bonaparte's position in France could not be secure until he had dealt with the Italian situation. In response, the First Consul led the Reserve Army over the snow on sledges made of hollowed-out logs. One of Bonaparte's Victories performs that amazing feat on a medal of 1800 (Br. 37), riding a cannon sledge over the Alps at breakneck speed.

84

FIRST CONSUL

Scargill's commentary,[2] remembering Hannibal's similar Alpine crossing, notes that 'Napoleon conducted his artillery over the spot on which his predecessor had lost his elephants.' The reverse of that medal shows the keys to the cities that Napoleon had won by this brilliant strategic move.

Once in Italy, however, Napoleon's strategy was less than brilliant. Having manoeuvred his army into an impossible situation at Marengo, he was saved by the skill of General Kellerman and by the timely arrival of Desaix, who was mortally wounded in the victorious charge. The death of Desaix steals from the Republican heroes the glory due to them.[3]

The honours heaped on the brave Desaix – a statue, a monument on the St Bernard, and several medals – were richly deserved. Two medals reproduce the scene of Desaix's death. The large 60mm uniface in lead by Andrieu has a beautifully engraved panel beneath the First Consul's portrait, that clearly shows the clash of armies with the death of Desaix in the centre. Even more remarkable is the 25mm piece by Brenet, picturing the monument to Desaix on Mount St Bernard. The scene of Desaix's death is exquisitely engraved on a panel that is remarkably small.

Napoleon claimed his share of the victory at Marengo on a medal with his portrait (Br. 38). The reverse is inscribed with the words he claims to have spoken to his troops in the midst of the battle; 'Soldiers, remember that it is my habit to sleep on the battlefield!'

Desaix's medal (Br. 44) of the same design, his bust replacing that of Bonaparte, is used to record his dying words. On the reverse: 'Go tell the first Consul that I leave with the regret of not having done enough to live in posterity.' The authenticity of both these dramatic messages is open to question.[4]

▼ **BATTLE OF MARENGO** (14 June 1800). The decisive battle of the Second Italian Campaign – nearly lost by Bonaparte but saved by the timely arrival of Desaix and the cavalry charge of Kellerman. Bust of Bonaparte with flags and military paraphernalia around a panel with the death of Desaix, the decisive moment of the battle. Though shown at the same size here, this medal is far larger than the one to the left. (Andrieu; Br. 40), lead *cliché*, 67mm.

◄ **MONUMENT TO DESAIX** (1805) on Mount St Bernard. The scene of Desaix's death exquisitely engraved by Brenet on this miniature medal. The pictorial panel itself measures only 7x9mm. (Br. 426), 26mm.

NAPOLEON'S MEDALS: *Victory to the Arts*

The Cisalpine Republic that Napoleon had formed out of much of northern Italy after the First Italian Campaign could now be reconstituted with the signing of the Convention of Alessandria the day after the battle. A medal by Lavy after Appiani's design (Br. 42) shows Hercules, having laid aside his club and lion skin, raising a recumbent Cisalpine Republic (or Italy). The Cisalpine Republic was soon incorporated into the new Kingdom of Italy. On a shield behind, Victory inscribes *HOSTIBUS PROPE MARENGUM FUSIS*. In the distance to the right is the rising sun with Napoleon's star at the centre.

On his victorious return from Italy Bonaparte stopped at Lyons where (on 29 June) he sponsored the rebuilding of the city centre, destroyed in the revolution against the Convention in the Year III (1793), laying the first stone of the reconstruction. 'The First Consul then placed the stone in which had been placed a casket of lead in which had been enclosed the medal in bronze that had been struck during the night.' The medal read in part, 'To Bonaparte, Rebuilder of Lyon, Verinac, Prefect. In the name of the grateful Lyonais.'[5]

BONAPARTE AT MARENGO (1800). Creation of a legend. The First Consul declares: 'Soldiers, remember that it is my habit to sleep on the battlefield.' His comment is engraved on the reverse of the medal. (Brenet and Auguste; Br. 38), 50mm.

DEATH OF DESAIX AT MARENGO (1800). Bonaparte immortalised Desaix with statues, a quay on the Seine and a funerary monument on Mount St Bernard. His improbable dying words are written on the reverse of the medal: 'Go and tell the First Consul that I die regretting having done too little to live to posterity.' (Brenet and Auguste; Br. 44)

86

FIRST CONSUL

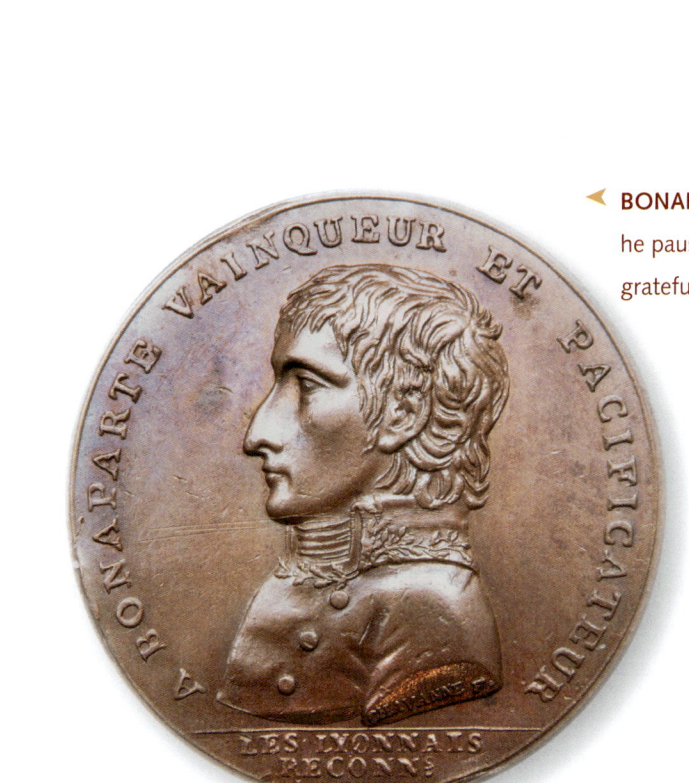

◄ **BONAPARTE AT LYONS** (1800). Returning victorious from Marengo, he pauses at Lyons to aid in rebuilding the the city. 'The Lyonais are grateful.' (Chauvanne; Br. 59)

▲ **BONAPARTE LAYS THE FIRST STONE** (1800) in the rebuilding of the centre of the city, destroyed in the revolt against the Convention in the Year III. (Chauvanne; Br. 59)

This medal was done by Mercie; another was struck later by Chavanne, very much in the image of the one he had done three years earlier, but with the hair a little shorter (Br. 59). This attention to Lyons, as to no other city in France (outside of Paris), suggests a special relationship with, or affection for, that place on the part of the First Consul.

Bonaparte wrote to his fellow consuls from Lyon,[6] explaining his delay in arriving at Paris, but expressing his satisfaction at beginning 'the restoration of that place, which I have seen so beautiful and which is now so shocking'. He eventually arrived in Paris in time to observe the grand festival.

Notes

1   Henin 923, pp.656–657.
2   p.12.
3   *Le Moniteur*, 22 June 1800, has an account of the battle.
4   *Le Moniteur*, 22 June 1800. J.M. Thompson believes that Desiax was killed instantly, leaving no time for a valedictory message. J.M. Thompson, *Napoleon Bonaparte, His Rise and Fall*, pp.163–164.
5   *Le Moniteur*, 6 July 1800.
6   Corresp. 4954.

VIII

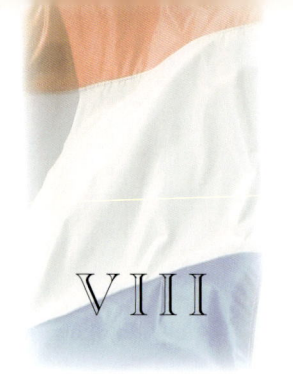

14 July 1800

The events of 18 Brumaire bring a new day to France, but this medal really looks forward to the celebration of 14 July (25 Messidor) in the next year. On that day the citizens who had given their lives for their country would be honoured. Bonaparte had issued a decree on 20 March that a column should be erected in the chief place of each department on which the names of those heroes would be displayed.[1] Two columns would be erected in Paris, one in the *Place Vendôme* and the other in the *Place de la Concorde*.

Marengo, however, had changed the focus of the celebration. Bonaparte had written from Milan a few days after the battle, in response to a tentative programme from Lucien, with some very specific requirements.[2] He wanted Garat or Fontaine to perform the funeral oration for Desaix which must be 'extremely well done'.

For his own victories he wanted composed a piece in Italian 'on the deliverance of the Cisalpine and Liguria and the glory of our arms'. He suggested for soloists performing with the choirs two divas known to Berthier, Madame Billington or Madame Grassini, 'who are the most famous virtuosi of Italy. Have composed, therefore, a beautiful piece in Italian' it should be played by a good orchestra and 'the tone of voice of these actresses must be known to the Italian composers.'

The account of the celebration in *Le Moniteur* shows that Lucien and his assistants had done their job extremely well, in view of the disparate elements that had to be integrated into the ceremonies. We find Madam Grassini, the diva Bonaparte had wanted, with Citizen Bianchi, singing 'the glory of those armies who had brought peace to their country … Who could better celebrate Marengo!'[3]

The medal for the National Column (Br. 61), at the *Place de la Concorde,* has Duvivier's portrait of Bonaparte with the other two consuls each relegated to a line of script beneath. The laying of the first stone was Lucien's province as Minister of the Interior. Lucien's speech ended with the promise that the column would 'have an existence as durable as the glory of the brave men who had founded, sustained and honoured the Republic'. The irony of that promise is that the column never proceeded beyond the first stone. Under the stone was placed Duvivier's medal along with those struck for Marengo.[4]

18 BRUMAIRE (1799). The rising sun dissipates the clouds. On 9–10 November 1799, Bonaparte seized power, creating an executive of three Consuls, an arrangement confirmed later by the Constitution of the Year VIII. This medal was really struck for the celebration of 14 July 1800, intended to honour the fallen heroes of the Republic. (Mercie; Br. 57), 61mm.

NAPOLEON'S MEDALS: *'Victory to the Arts'*

NATIONAL COLUMN

(1800). Ordered as a monument to French heroes who had died in defence of the Republic, the Column was never built. The medal and columns were authorized in March 1800. The first and only stone was laid at the anniversary celebration of the Fall of the Bastille, but the heroes of the Republic were soon forgotten. The National Column and the Column of the Department of the Seine eventually evolved into the Column of the Grand Army in the *Place Vendôme*. (Duvivier; Br. 61)

The programme for the column for the Department of the Seine, to be set up in the *Place Vendôme,* featured the Prefect of that Department, Nicolas Th. B. Frochot. Frochot had a distinguished career in the period of the Revolution and came to his office at about the 18 Brumaire. The programme in which he was to lay the first stone was outlined in *Le Moniteur* on the day before the celebration.[5] The column was to be in honour of the 'heroes of the Department of the Seine who had died defending their country and for liberty.' It should be set up in the centre of the *Place Vendôme*. The ground was to be prepared for the column by the removal of the existing pedestal and other materials. Prefect Frochot would then lay the first stone.

A medal was also ordered, 6cm in diameter, with the busts of the three consuls and on the reverse the appropriate inscriptions. The medal which appeared some two weeks later was exactly as ordered (Br. 64).[6] It featured conjoined portraits of the three consuls and in the exergue a reference to the Constitution of the Year VIII, which was the legal basis of their power. On the reverse was a dedication of the Department of the Seine, in *LA GUERRE DE LA LIBERTE* to *SES BRAVES* and a statement that Th. B. Frochot had laid the first stone of the monument.

14 JULY 1800

LAYING THE FIRST STONE. (Reverse of Br. 61) According to the inscription, Lucien Bonaparte, then Minister of the Interior, laid the first stone on 14 July 1800.

In *Le Moniteur* of 31 July Frochot expressed his appreciation to Gatteaux, the engraver, and his admiration for the medal: 'such perfection. Resemblance, expression, distinctness of character; see that which the experts have noted and applauded …' The editor of *Le Moniteur* agreed that 'the sight of that medal confirms the eulogies contained in the letter of the Prefect of the Department of the Seine.'

This was the beginning of a long and distinguished career as Prefect for Frochot. He presided over numerous improvements to his city – buildings, fountains, the Ourq Canal – and received many honours from Bonaparte, until he lost his position in 1812 following the General Mallet conspiracy. There was a long account of the investigation into Frochot's conduct in the 25 December 1812 issue of the *Le Moniteur* that showed him to be more unfortunate and unwise than disloyal.

There is a significant phrase in the programme for the celebration that is prophetic. When the first stone had been placed, *Le Moniteur* noted that the continuation of the work would be suspended 'until the model of the column is adopted'. Quarrels about the form of the monument, which can be followed in *Le Moniteur*, soon doomed the project. Neither of the Paris columns proceeded beyond the first stone, until Denon and Bonaparte revived the plan several years

COLUMN OF THE DEPARTMENT OF THE SEINE (14 July 1800). Designed to record the names of the heroes who died fighting for liberty. Lucien Bonaparte was Minister of the Interior when the first stone was laid, but Frochot, Prefect of the Department of the Seine, managed to get his name on the medal. According to *Le Moniteur*, he was very much pleased with it. (N. Gatteau; Br. 64), 60mm.

14 JULY 1800

later, turning it into the Column of the *Place Vendôme,* in honour of the Grand Army of the campaign of 1805. So much for Republican heroes!

Monuments in the other departments suffered the same fate, though several medals were produced reporting the placing of the first stone by the Prefect of the Department. These included a medal for the Department of the Seine and Marne for which Prefect Laroche Foucalt is said to have placed the first stone.

Fontanes did not, as Bonaparte suggested, perform the funeral oration for Desaix, but he did something far more effective. He wrote a poem set to music, performed by three orchestras and sung by choir and soloists in the Temple of Mars.[7] The *Moniteur* reported that the performance was interrupted many times by applause and the audience reacted with profound feeling to the words '*Tu muers brave Desaix!*'[8]

One of the principal features of the tribute to Desaix was the dedication of the *Quai Desaix,* at which Lucien delivered a speech and laid another first stone and for which a medal was struck[9]. There was, apparently, insufficient time to design and engrave a medal worthy of the brave Desaix. The result was a plain medal,

STATUS OF DESAIX (1810). Erected ten years after his death at Marengo, it showed the Emperor's continuing affection for the hero, but proved an embarrassment. Eventually the statue was melted down, along with Chaudet's statue of Napoleon on top of the monument in the *Place Vendôme,* to provide metal for a statue of Henry IV. (Brenet; Br. 976)

COLUMN OF THE DEPARTMENT OF THE SEINE AND MARNE (14 July 1800). This was another abortive attempt to follow Bonaparte's instructions. As in the other columns inaugurated on this day, the Prefect of the Department laid the first stone and the project was abandoned. (Br. 66)

FOUNDATION OF THE *QUAI DESAIX* (14 July 1800). There was not time to prepare a proper medal for the real hero of the celebration, the dead Desaix, so a medal with only a simple inscription and a ceremony inaugurating the *Quai Desaix* had to suffice, Minister of the Interior Lucien Bonaparte presiding. However, a very moving Cantata was performed in his honour. (Br. 68)

unsigned, consisting of simple inscriptions, with the names of the consuls and Lucien on one side and date and purpose of the dedication on the other. Lucien's speech was short and to the point, ending with a hope more likely to be fulfilled than the promise made to the Republican heroes of the National Column: 'May this *quai* last as long as the memory of Desaix!'

Napoleon's final tribute to Desaix was a statue set up in 1810 that proved an embarrassment (Br. 976). The outstretched arm of the statue seemed to be pointing across the street at a haberdasher's shop, as if to say, 'Will someone bring me a suit of clothes?' Eventually the statue was melted down along with Chaudet's statue of the Emperor Napoleon on top of the Column of the *Place Vendôme*, to provide metal for the equestrian statue of Henry IV.

A. Jourdan complained, in *Le Moniteur* of 14 July, that the anniversary of the fall of the Bastille had nearly been forgotten and rejoiced that 'there will be celebrated a second time in a manner worthy of it, the first, the most beautiful days of the revolution!'

Jourdan must have been disappointed to find scant mention of such a celebration in later issues of the journal. We may suppose 'that glorious day' had again been forgotten. What *Le Moniteur* did report, year after year, were regular celebrations of Napoleon's birthday all over France. Fortuitously, the birthday of an obscure saint, St Napoleon, fell on a day very close to Bonaparte's birthday so that the two could be celebrated at the same time.

Notes

1 Corresp. 4683.
2 Corresp. 4938.
3 *Le Moniteur,* 17 July 1800
4 *Le Moniteur* 17 July 1800 records Lucien's speech.
5 *Le Moniteur* 14 July 1800.
6 *Le Moniteur* 21 July 1800.
7 *Le Moniteur* 16 July 1800.
8 *Le Moniteur* 17 July 1800.
9 *Le Moniteur* 17 July 1800.

IX

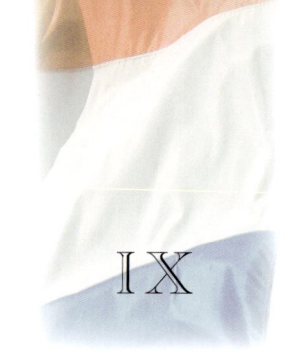

England – Peace and War

The Treaty of Luneville, signed on 9 February 1801, ended the war between France and Austria. France was again the master of northern Italy, although Austria retained Venice and the Adriatic coast, Istria and Dalmatia. The Peace was celebrated on a medal by Andrieu; a lovely Peace Maiden stands holding a cornucopia and an olive branch. A medal by Droz (Br. 106, p.52) expresses the broader and truer picture. The sun shines brightly on the continent while a cloud envelops England. France was still at war with England and remained so through long and difficult negotiations that ended, finally, with the Peace of Amiens, signed on 25 March 1802.

A medal dated 10 June 1801, during the period before the Peace of Amiens, illustrates Napoleon's shrewd diplomacy and bears indirectly on the United States' Louisiana Purchase of 1803. The medal is dedicated to Louis, 'King of Etruria', the reverse is a dedication to his Queen, Marie Louise Josephine. The occasion is a visit of King Louis and Queen Marie Louise of Etruria (formerly Tuscany) to Paris to receive their crown from the hand of Bonaparte.

The background to this event was the treaty of St Idolfonso on 7 October 1800 between France and Charles IV, King of Spain, by which he agreed to exchange title to Louisiana for Tuscany, to be renamed Etruria and given to his son-in-law, Louis.[1] Louis, son of the aged Duke of Parma, was married to the Spanish King's daughter, Marie Louise. This deal, which seems to us a bad bargain, appealed to the King of Spain as a re-establishment of the Bourbon presence in northern Italy, but ignored the real seat of power in that country.

The young sovereigns were royally feted in France for a month. It soon became apparent to Bonaparte, however, as General Savary noted, that the king of Etruria was weak and irresponsible, interested only in trivial pursuits and incapable of ruling a kingdom.[2] Savary reported that on his departure

PEACE OF LUNEVILLE

(1801). Andrieu's maiden holds an olive branch and cornucopia celebrating the peace with Austria signed on 9 February 1801, which made France again master of northern Italy. (Andrieu; Br. 107)

ENGLAND – PEACE AND WAR

VISIT OF THE KING AND QUEEN OF ETRURIA TO PARIS (10 June 1801). King Louis and Queen Maria Louise Josephine visit Paris to receive from Bonaparte the crown of the Kingdom of Etruria (formerly Tuscany), which the King of Spain had received for his daughter and son-in-law in exchange for Louisiana; a poor exchange, since Bonaparte reserved the real power in Etruria for himself. For Louis, a sword, a book of laws and scales for justice, symbolic of the intruments of power he never wielded. For the Queen, the Genius of France offers her a rose. (Dupre; Br.152), AE gilt. 34mm.

for Etruria (Tuscany), Bonaparte remarked, 'Rome may rest easy, he will never cross the Rubicon.' Bonaparte sent along one of his generals as ambassador to Etruria, but actually 'advisor' and the real ruler in the kingdom. A detachment of French troops ensured French control. The ironies of the medal, therefore, may easily be perceived; a sword over an open book inscribed *CODE TUSCAN*, a set of balances for justice, all on a *fasces*, the symbol of the Roman magistrate's authority – the symbols of a power never exercised.

NAPOLEON'S MEDALS: *Victory to the Arts*

CORNWALLIS AT AMIENS (1802). The Marquis Cornwallis 'Plenipotentiary at Amiens' was overmatched by Joseph Bonaparte and Napoleon and came away with a bad treaty, which everyone knew could not last. (Handcock; Br. 204)

POST NUBILA PHOEBUS. The rising sun shows a genie presenting a tablet to Britannia with the names of signatories to the treaty. Britannia holds a portrait of George III. This was not a 'Definitive Treaty', as the medal proclaims. (Br. 204)

On the reverse, the Genius of France, accompanied by the French cock, offers the Queen a rose, all she ever got from Bonaparte – after the month of parties. The Queen enjoyed the parties and Josephine's hospitality, but the French continued to rule her country even after Louis' death in 1804, Bonaparte refusing to withdraw his troops. Etruria was annexed to France in 1807.

As for Louisiana, Bonaparte at first thought of developing a French imperial presence there, supported from Santo Domingo, but the collapse of the latter, rising pressure from America against French occupation, and the fear that the French presence would drive the United States into the arms of Britain, led the First Consul to turn his back on Louisiana. He sold it to America in the spring of 1803. The text of the Treaty is in Napoleon's Correspondence.[3]

In England, the Treaty of Amiens and the return of peace were greeted with rejoicing. In France, Droz's beautiful medal, *LE RETOUR D'ASTREE* expressed the general feeling. Astrée, the heavenly star, peace and justice, descending again to earth.

The Treaty was clearly unfavourable to England, however, and the English knew it, though a medal proclaims it *A DEFINITIVE TREATY*. The Marquis Cornwallis, *BRITISH PLENIPOTENTIARY AT AMIENS*, was overmatched by Joseph Bonaparte and Napoleon. The French had the true picture. Napoleon as Mars, cradling Victory, extends an olive branch to a suppliant Britannia, leaning heavily on an unhappy British lion (Br. 195, p.47).

Meanwhile, Bonaparte was improving his position in Italy, turning the Cisalpine Republic into the Italian Republic, as a medal proclaims. Bonaparte was elected President of the new Republic.

RETURN OF ASTREE – PEACE OF AMIENS (1802). Justice returns to earth with balances and olive-entwined caduceus. The Peace of Amiens was signed on 25 March 1802 amid general rejoicing – an illusion as beautiful as Droz's engraving. The terms of the Treaty, unfavourable to England, made a new war inevitable.

(Droz; Br. 200)

CONSTITUTION OF THE ITALIAN REPUBLIC AT LYONS (January 1802). The Genius of Arts hands a tablet inscribed *COS ITALIC* to a woman representing the Cisalpine Republic. An infant Justice sits behind her. Bonaparte's diplomatic wizardry has transformed the Cisalpine Republic into the Italian Republic, of which he was elected president. A quotation from Horace promises eternal prosperity. An inscription on the reverse promises the same thing 'assured by the Constitution under the auspices of Bonaparte'. (Manfredini; Br. 189), 54mm.

ENGLAND – PEACE AND WAR

The French had no illusions about the duration of the peace. A small (14mm) piece, titled 'Armed for Peace', expresses the French point of view very well. On one side is a helmeted Bonaparte, on the reverse is Pliny's stork watchman standing on one leg, holding a stone in the other. An olive branch and a thunderbolt are in the field. Scargill's manuscript has it right:[4] 'A stork is seen holding a flint in its claw, as an emblem of that foreseeing vigilance which neither repose nor even sleep itself can surprise.'[5]

Unhappy with the French observance of the Treaty, Britain declared war on 27 May 1803. Scholars struggle to identify the strange looking creature which tears up the Treaty of Amiens on a medal dated May 1803. It ought to be the British lion, since the medal is Napoleon's comment on England's treacherous behaviour. Perhaps it is a leopard (Bramsen, Essling), an allusion to the leopards on the English coat of arms. Scargill's commentary sees 'a panther, the type of the English arms.' Captain Laskey of the British army remembering just three years after the end of the war his country's fierce and stubborn resistance to Bonaparte, may be forgiven for recognising 'an English Bulldog'.[6] The die break beneath *ROMPU* ('broken') is probably deliberate.

Bonaparte's first act was the easy conquest of Hanover on 3 June, featured on the reverse of the medal on which England broke the Treaty (Br. 271). Victory rides a swift horse into that last English possession on the continent, a blow to English pride and a way of closing the mouth of the German North Sea ports. Victory's choice of steed symbolised more than an easy conquest, for Hanover was famous for its fine horses, now made available to the French Army, the importance of which may be seen in the accounts of the French occupation in *Le Moniteur*. As mentioned earlier, the articles of capitulation are careful to specify that all of the horses of the army of Hanover, both cavalry and artillery, should be turned over to the French.[7]

A note early in August reports that the French Army is in a most satisfactory situation, having taken 4,000 horses from the Hanoverian army. '*Ces chevaux sont fort beaux!*'[8] Hanover was famous for the quality of its horses. An English medal in the Mudie series (Br. 1489), celebrating the British re-conquest of Hanover, shows a seated Britannia feeding a sheaf of barley to two horses (Br. 1489, p.199).

Napoleon's real concern now was the invasion of England, a plan considered and rejected in 1798 that now for the first time seemed possible with increased naval construction and the addition of the Spanish fleet. The plan was to ferry the army across the Channel on several thousand small boats while the French and Spanish fleets held the British navy at bay. Thus the 1804 medal of Hercules tying up the Nemean (British) Lion has as its legend: 'In the year XII 2000 boats were constructed.'

The focus was at Boulogne where Soult commanded the 'Army of England'. We see their encampment on the reverse of a medal dated 16 August 1804,

'ARMED FOR PEACE'
(1803). Napoleon in a helmet. On the reverse, a stork holding a stone (the 'watchman') with an olive branch and a thunderbolt in the field. (Br. 167), 14mm.

THE TREATY OF AMIENS BROKEN BY ENGLAND (1803). An English leopard (or lion, panther, or bulldog!) tears up the Treaty of Amiens. Is the die break under *ROMPU* deliberate? (Jeuffroy; Br. 271)

HERCULES TIES UP THE NEMEAN LION (1804) Also, of course, the British lion, preparing for the English invasion. The usual ancient scene shows the hero strangling the animal. '2000 boats have been built' boasts the inscription. This was a labour beyond the strength of Hercules. (Droz; Br. 320)

NAPOLEON'S MEDALS: *Victory to the Arts*

LEGIONARY HONOURS (1804). Napoleon in camp at Bologne, August 1804, preparing for the invasion of England. Seated on the curule chair, he distributes legionary crosses to four soldiers, representing four divisions of the army. (Chaudet; Jeuffroy; Br. 318)

which pictures Napoleon's distribution of crosses of the Legion of Honour to representatives of four divisions.[9] Napoleon, portrayed as a Roman magistrate, sits on the curule chair attended by two men in Roman dress. The soldiers receiving the honours are in uniform.

The medallion displaying the medal of honour itself is beautifully engraved by Jaley (Br. 310, see page 202). A double-rayed five-pointed star surrounded by oak and laurel branches around a circle with the words *HONNEUR ET PATRIE*. Within the circle is a delicately engraved eagle holding a thunderbolt in its talons. Around the edge the claim *AUSPICE NEAPOLEONE GALLIA RENOVATA*. The Legion of Honour was proposed in May of 1802 with an elaborate organisation[10] and broke with tradition in including worthy civilians

ENGLAND – PEACE AND WAR

as well as military heroes. The inauguration and the first distribution of the decorations took place in the Temple of Mars on 15 July 1804.

In 1814, Louis XVIII reorganised the Legion of Honour. The general dissatisfaction, particularly among the old soldiers, may be the reason the eagle returning from Elba carries in its beak the original Legion of Honour (Br. 1482).

The failure of Napoleon to concentrate his navy in the Channel at the right time in the summer of 1805 doomed his hope for a successful invasion of England. By 3 September of that year the threat and the opportunity provided by a belligerent Austria persuaded Napoleon to abandon the attempt and to embark on the campaign that led to Austerlitz (Br. 430). The Battle of Trafalgar in October sealed the fate of the flotilla in the Channel ports.

A medal showing Hercules subduing Antaeus, with the boast 'Struck in London in 1804' (Br. 364), is symbolic of Napoleon's failure. The medal was never struck,

PLAN OF THE CAMP AT BOULOGNE (1804). The arrangement by corps. 80,000 men of the Army of England, under Marshal Soult, take the oath to the Emperor. Strangely, the medal was not struck until 1806, when the army was no longer there. (Jaley; Br. 318)

of course. The English obtained a copy and had great fun with it after the war (Br. 2188). (Antaeus, who derives his strength from being in contact with the earth, was perhaps a clumsy choice to represent the nation that would triumph so comprehensively at Trafalgar.)

In November of 1806, at the time of the Berlin Decree announcing the Continental System to cut off British products from European markets, an attempt was made to reuse the medal to symbolise the blockade of England. The words *DESCENTE EN ANGLETERRE* were replaced with *TOTOS DIVISOS ORBE BRITANNOS* ('The British cut off from the whole world'). The same die was used; the remnant of the original inscription is visible beneath the Latin quotation from Virgil.[11]

Notes

1 John Holland Rose, *The Life of Napoleon I*, London, G.Bell and Sons, Ltd., Tenth Edition, 1929, pp.364–372.

2 *Mémoirs de Duc de Rovigo*, Paris, 1828. Vol. 1, p.364.

3 Corresp. 6706. April 23, 1803.

4 pp.14–15.

5 The reference is to Pliny, *Natural History*, Loeb, vol. 3, 10:30. Describing the behaviour of cranes in Africa: 'At night, sentries hold a stone in their claws which if drowsiness make them drop it, it falls and convicts them of slackness, while the rest sleep with their head tucked under their wing, standing on either foot by turns.' The guardian crane became a part of medieval heraldry and is found on coats of arms. (Arthur Charles Fox-Davies, *A Complete Guide to Heraldry,* 1909, p.247.)

6 Captain J.C. Laskey, *A Description of the Series of Medals Struck at the National Medal Mint by Order of Napoleon Bonaparte*. London: H.R. Young, 1818, p.57.

7 *Le Moniteur,* 14 July 1803.

8 14 August 1803.

9 As the medal was not struck until 1806 when the Grand Army was no longer there, perhaps Napoleon had not given up the idea, or at least wanted the people to think that it was still possible.

10 Corresp. 6083.

11 *First Eclogue 65*. Edwards 14:17.

X

Napoleon – Emperor and King

Napoleon's coronation medal, for the event that took place on 2 December 1804, is another appeal to history and the ancient world. The Emperor stands raised on a shield in imperial garb holding a sceptre and wearing the sword of Charlemagne.[1] Elevation on a shield is an old Frankish custom reported of Clovis, the founder of the Merovingian kingdom.[2] Holding the Emperor aloft are a Roman Senator and a French farmer. In the field is a book inscribed 'Law' for the Senator, with a plowshare for the farmer. 70,000 miniature versions in silver (14mm) were struck to be thrown to the crowds.[3]

Count Philippe de Ségur, son of the Count de Ségur, Grand Master of Ceremonies for Napoleon, relates a curious incident concerning the sword of Charlemagne – a human touch amid so much artificial pageantry.[4] As a young man, Ségur was given charge of the imperial insignia, including Charlemagne's sword, the night before the ceremony. He relates that the officer under him to whom he had entrusted the sword 'was foolish enough to draw it against one of his comrades, who having vainly parried with his own sabre, congratulated himself on having been overcome and slightly wounded by the sword of so great a man.'

A private coronation issue by Merlen (Br. 333) is extravagant in design and inscription. Four warriors lift the Emperor, in elaborate imperial costume, on a shield. In the field to the left is a cannon. On the right a hydra spits daggers. To the Emperor is attributed *BONTE DE TITUS SAGESSE DE M. AURELE GENIE DE CHARLES M*. The inscription in the exergue explains the hostility of the hydra. 'At the name of the greatest of heroes the British hydra trembles.' There are more extravagant titles on the reverse. Another private issue (Br. 335) attempts to put Napoleon in the tradition of Caesar by repeating his famous saying: over his laurel crowned bust is inscribed *NAPOLEON VENIT VIDET VINCIT*.

The anointing of the Emperor was originally planned for the week before the coronation actually occurred, but the Pope was unable to make it in time so that the anointing and coronation had to be combined. Napoleon's letters reveal his anxiety that the Pope might be late.[5]

CORONATION OF NAPOLEON (1804). 2 December 1804. The Emperor is raised on a shield by a Roman Senator and a French farmer-soldier, reflecting an old Frankish custom applied to Clovis. An open book reads *LOIS, LOIS* ('Laws, laws'), for the Senator. The ploughshare belongs to the farmer. (Chaudet; Jeuffroy; Br. 326)

SMALL CORONATION MEDAL. A 13mm silver piece, smallest of four denominations struck for the Coronation. The irregular flan results from striking without a collar. Denon reported to the Emperor on 4 January 1805 (AN 27) that 70,000 had been struck. They were thrown in great numbers to the crowd. (Br. 329)

108

The story that Napoleon seized the crown from the Pope's hands and crowned himself appears to be untrue, though it is true that he crowned himself. After the Pope had blessed the crowns and other regalia and returned them to the altar, Napoleon took the crown, a laurel wreath of gold, and placed it on his own head. He then took the crown for Josephine, first holding it over his own head, stating that he crowned Josephine as his wife, not in her own right, and then crowned her. This is the moment preserved in David's famous painting.

Napoleon was undoubtedly aware of events a thousand years earlier in the pontificate of Leo III. In that era Charlemagne clearly held the upper hand in the age-long struggle between Pope and Emperor – except for one brilliant move on Leo's part. On Christmas day in the year 800, while Charlemagne was kneeling in the church at prayer, Pope Leo III approached him unawares from behind and crowned him Emperor. Charlemagne was furious afterwards, in part we may be sure because Leo's act made it appear that Charlemagne owed his crown to the Pope. Napoleon would not let that happen to the new Charlemagne.

On a medal dedicated to Pope Pius VII, with the Coronation date, and presented to him on 8 January on his visit to the Medal Mint, the Pope is called *HOSPES NEOPOLIONIS IMP*, a phrase with no little irony in view of Napoleon's treatment of him. But this reluctant guest made good use of his time in Paris, remaining four months in the capital. He visited the holy places, said mass in Notre Dame, held audiences for the faithful in the Louvre, was received and escorted with pomp at Versailles and visited the Sèvres porcelain and Gobelin tapestry factories. At the Museum of Natural History he listened to a Latin discourse on the glory of God in nature by the Director of the *Jardin des Plantes*. He toured the gallery, showing his lively interest by the questions he addressed to his guides.[6]

The Pope's visit to the Medal Mint, as to the Natural History Museum, is notable for the vitality of his interest in the variety of things he observed. The report of the visit also tells us a good deal about the workings and organisation of the Mint itself.

> He examined in the greatest detail all the operations which preceded the minting of medals, that is to say, the forges, the rollers, the cutters for the preparation of the flans. Arriving at the minting presses, the first medal in gold to be struck, was presented to him by M. Denon, Director of the Medal Mint, representing His Holiness crowned with the tiara and dressed in the pontifical habit, with this legend, *PIUS VII, p.M. HOSPES NAPOLEONIS, IMP …*

The reverse is an inscription noting the visit to the Mint. The second medal presented to the Pope was that pictured previously (Br. 350), with the Cathedral of Notre Dame on the reverse. After the presentation

POPE PIUS VII AT PARIS (1804). *HOSPES NEAPOLIONIS IMP.* ('Guest of the Emperor Napoleon'). The words are both ironic and prophetic. The Pope was a 'guest' in Paris for the coronation, but on Napoleon's orders, and in 1809 he was imprisoned when he defied the Emperor. (Droz; Br. 350)

NOTRE DAME DE PARIS (1804). Scene of the Coronation. *IMPERATOR SACRATUS.* Napoleon insisted that he be consecrated, not crowned, by the Pope. Napoleon took the crown, turned his back on the Pope, and himself placed the crown on his head, avoiding the mistake of Charlemagne, who allowed Pope Leo to crown him. (Jaley; Br. 350)

110

NAPOLEON – EMPEROR AND KING

The minting of the first two medals continued and His Holiness distributed them to all his entourage … Afterwards the Director conducted him into the room where are kept all the dies and punches of the medals struck in France from Louis XII up to the Emperor Napoleon. His holiness viewed with a lively interest that rich collection, perhaps unique, or at least the most notable in Europe.

On the day after the Coronation, 3 December 1804, the Emperor distributed the new eagle standards to the troops on the *Champ de Mars,* and received the oath of the Army. The scene is pictured on a medal and the ceremony described in *Le Moniteur.*[7] At the height of the ceremony the Emperor addressed his troops:

> Soldiers, behold your standards! Those eagles will always remain the focus of your allegiance, wherever your Emperor decides it is necessary for the defence of his throne and his people.

The magnificent imperial eagle, laurel crowned and seated on a mountain top, presiding over coronation festivities later that month expresses the spirit evoked by the new standards: *FIXA PERENNIS IN ALTO SEDES* ('His seat is fixed forever at the summit').

DISTRIBUTION OF THE EAGLES (1804). On 3 December 1804, the day after the coronation, Napoleon distributed the new Eagle Standards to the troops on the *Champ de Mars*. The Imperial Eagle became the symbol of the advancing French army. (Jeuffroy; Br. 357), 27mm.

NAPOLEON'S MEDALS: *Victory to the Arts*

THE IMPERIAL EAGLE. Laurel-crowned and seated on a mountain top, the eagle presides over coronation festivities. 'His seat is fixed forever at the summit' reads the inscription. (Brenet; Br. 359), 36mm.

CORONATION FESTIVITIES (1804) at the City Hall, 16 December 1804. Not the best likeness of Josephine. (Brenet; Br. 359)

Several medals were struck to celebrate the coronation festivities later in the month. Two of these are for the banquet given at the *Hotel de Ville* on 16 December. The smaller medal may have been intended for distribution to guests at the banquet. On the obverse are the conjoined heads of Napoleon and Josephine, on the reverse the imperial eagle described above.

A large medal (69mm) struck for the same event and signed by the artist Prudhon as well as the engraver, Romain-Vincent Jeuffroy, shows the Emperor in Roman costume, seated on the Roman Magistrate's curule chair receiving the city of Paris in audience. Behind the lady representing the city is a ship in which a cherub, the

NAPOLEON – EMPEROR AND KING

genius of the city, holds the steering oar, his eyes fixed on Napoleon's star in the heavens. *TUTELA PRAESENS* ('Present protection') is promised.

The decorations, the ceremonies, the interminable speeches and the poems set to music of that celebration are elaborately described in *Le Moniteur*. Coronation celebrations were staged throughout the Empire. Napoleon showed the same care for the proper symbolism at his coronation in Milan on 26 May 1805, as King of Italy. A medal shows Italy crowning Napoleon with the Iron Crown of the Lombards. The Emperor holds the sword of Charlemagne in his left hand and holds his right above an altar on which is placed the constitution. As in Notre Dame, Napoleon crowned himself.

CORONATION FESTIVITIES (1804). A grand medal signed by the great artist, Prudhon, as designer. Napoleon is in Roman costume, seated on the curule chair, attended by the City of Paris. The ship of the city behind is guided by her Genius, whose eye is fixed on Napoleon's star above. *TUTELA PRAESENS* ('present protection') is assured. (Prudhon; Jeuffroy; Br. 358), 68mm.

CORONATION IN MILAN (1805). Italy crowns Napoleon king with the Iron Crown of the Lombards (26 May 1805). He extends his right hand above an altar on which is placed the constitution. A helmet and a caduceus are in the field. As in the coronation ceremony at Paris, Napoleon himself placed the crown on his head. (Manfredini; Br. 420)

NAPOLEON'S MEDALS: *Victory to the Arts*

IRON CROWN OF THE LOMBARDS (1805). In taking the crown of Agilulfus, the Lombard king, uniting France and Italy, Napoleon portrayed himself as the heir of Charlemagne, who had done the same thing. (Jaley; Br. 418)

Another medal pictures the crown of Agilulfus, the ancient Lombard king (592–615), a circlet of gold and jewels over an iron ring, said to have been forged from one of the nails that had pierced Christ's hand. The inscription reads: *AGILULFUS. GRATIA. DEI. GLORIOSUS. REX*. The crown was brought from the cathedral of Monza to Milan by an escort of the Guard and of citizens of Monza.[8] Napoleon was following in the footsteps of Charlemagne who in 774 had conquered the Lombards and assumed the title 'King of the Lombards'. As he placed the crown on his head, Napoleon spoke the traditional words of the Lombard ceremony, 'God has given it to me; let him beware who touches it!'[9] Napoleon was now Emperor of France and King of Italy.

Notes

1. Napoleon had taken the sword from Charlemagne's tomb at Aix-la-Chapelle. General Count de Ségur, *Memoirs of an Aide-de Camp of Napoleon 1800–1812*, revised by his grandson, trans. by H.A. Patchett-Martin. New York, 1895, p.136.
2. Gregory of Tours, *History of the Franks*, II, 40.
3. Denon's report to the Emperor, 4 January 1805. (AN 27).
4. De Ségur, p.136.
5. E.g. Corresp. 8161. 'It is therefore indispensable that the Pope hasten his journey.'
6. *Le Moniteur*, 10 January 1805.
7. Ibid.
8. *Le Moniteur*, 1 June 1805.
9. The first phrase of this declaration, so appropriate to Bonaparte, actually appears on a companion medal, Br. 423.

XI

Austerlitz and Aftermath

On a medal celebrating Napoleon's victory at Austerlitz (2 December 1805), Victory blows her trumpet and stands on a pile of the spoil from an earlier battle sent as a gift to the Mayors of Paris. The reverse of the medal shows the visit of the Mayors of Paris received by Napoleon and Murat.

The story of the medal's origin involves the otherwise fruitless Commission of the Academy. On 14 August 1806 the Commission met in extraordinary session to consider a request of the Prefect of the Department of the Seine for a medal describing the visit of the Mayors of Paris to Napoleon to thank him for the gift of standards and cannon taken from the enemy at Wertingen, 10 October 1805.

Visconti, one of the commissioners, read a proposal to the Commission. On one side would be Victory blowing her trumpet 'of renown' and holding in her hand the letter from his majesty, *IMP. URBAE SUE* ('The Emperor to his City'). On the other side would be the delegation presenting the letter of gratitude for the standards to Napoleon and Murat.

The proposal was adopted to the letter, including the branch of laurel and the platform on which Napoleon and Murat stood. The strange armour that they wore resembled 'that of Francis I recovered at Vienna'. The nymph from the fountain at Schoenbrunn is 'at their feet. The name "Schoenbrunn" can be read on the edge of the urn that contained the water.' The Commission decided to adopt Visoconti's proposal and assigned Lamot to do the drawing and Brenet and Galle the engraving. The 68mm medal was struck at the Paris Mint.[1]

But this was an epilogue; a great deal of history preceded the visit of the Mayors to Schoenbrunn. At the end of August 1805, Napoleon abandoned the camp at Bologne when threatened by a new coalition of Austria, Russia, and Britain (Br. 430). The First Austrian Campaign that followed was the subject of a series of medals, planned and executed under the direction of Denon, most during the year 1806.[2]

Moving with amazing speed against the Austrians, Napoleon caught General Mack at Ulm and forced his surrender. One medal, the 'Address on the Lech Bridge' is a comment on the early phase of this campaign, apparently an actual event, but also a reflection of a familiar scene from antiquity, the Roman general haranguing his troops. On 12 October 1805, a few days before Mack's surrender

NAPOLEON'S MEDALS: *Victory to the Arts*

◄ FAME BLOWS HER TRUMPET (1805), standing on enemy cannon and standards taken at the Battle of Austerlitz, Napoleon's most brilliant victory. In her hand is an unrolled scroll, reading *IMP URBI SUAE*. On the other side is a delegation of Mayors of Paris, thanking Napoleon for a gift of standards from a previous battle. The Paris Mayors asked the Commission for a medal celebrating their visit. Visconti responded with a design that was drawn by Lemot and engraved by Brenet. (Lemot; Brenet; Br. 453), 68mm.

THE MAYORS OF PARIS AT SCHOENBRUNN ► (13 December 1805). Napoleon with Murat in curious armour receives the Mayors of Paris at Schoenbrunn who have come to thank him for the gift to the city of cannon and standards from the Battle of Wertingen (8 October). Napoleon promised to send standards taken from the Russians at Austerlitz to be placed in the Church of Notre Dame. A medal of the city of Paris, proposed by Visconti of the French Academy, designed by the sculptor Lemot and engraved by Galle. (Lemot; Galle; Br. 453), 68mm.

at Ulm, the Emperor addressed his tired and dispirited soldiers, weary from the arduous march from the Channel. Napoleon spoke to them of the prospects before them, 'the imminence of a great battle', and his confidence in them. This took place during terrible weather and the troops 'suffered from extreme cold, but the Emperor's words were of fire; while listening to him, the soldier forgot his fatigue and his privations, and became impatient for the arrival of the hour of combat.'[3]

'Antiquity offers many works representing a similar subject, such as Caesar, Trajan and Marcus Aurelius haranguing their armies' wrote Vivant Denon to the Emperor when describing a similar scene as the subject for a painting. Probably Denon was the source for the design of this medal also.[4]

AUSTERLITZ AND AFTERMATH

Marshal Ney's recovery of the French standards at Innsbruch on 7 November – which had been lost in a previous war – is also the subject of a medal. The Emperor stands in Roman military dress, holding the standards in one hand and a Victory in the other. According to the Twenty-fifth Grand Army Bulletin from Schoenbrunn, when Ney returned the standards to the Army, 'tears ran down the eyes of all the old soldiers … For his colours the French soldier has a sentiment partaking of tenderness; they are the objects of his worship, like a present received from the hands of a mistress.'[5] The Emperor ordered that touching scene to be memorialised in a painting, and Denon also saw that it was worthy of a medal.

Two medals celebrated the capture of Vienna on 13 November. On one (Br. 443, p.44) Napoleon, as Hercules, receives the submission of two females, representing the cities of Vienna and Pressburg, each presenting him with a key. Perhaps, as David Block suggests, the Emperor 'is not accepting the proffered keys; he is looking for new conquests. The approaching Russian allies of the Austrians have yet to be defeated.'[6] The other medallion, by the Italian engraver Luigi Manfredini (Br. 444, p.24), is a beautiful adaptation of the ancient captive maiden with trophy theme. The trophy in the scene is constructed of Austrian arms, a point made

ADDRESS ON THE LECH BRIDGE (1805). Abandoning his plan to invade England, Napoleon led the Army eastward to meet a new Austrian threat. After a long and difficult march and in terrible weather, he addressed the dispirited army and the soldiers forgot their fatigue and swore an oath to conquer. All are in Roman dress, copying a familiar ancient scene. (Zix; Andireu; Br. 432)

117

NAPOLEON'S MEDALS: *'Victory to the Arts'*

FRENCH INSIGNIA RECOVERED (1805). Napoleon in Roman military dress, holding in one hand a statue of Victory and in the other a standard with a statue of Jupiter. On 7 November 1805, Marshal Ney, entering Innsbruck, discovered standards lost in the previous war in an arsenal. When the standards were returned to the regiment, 'tears ran down the eyes of all the old soldiers'. (Brenet; Br. 442)

clear by the double-headed Austrian eagle on the shield and 'F.II' for the Emperor, Francis II. The obverse of this medal (Br. 444) is as ridiculous as the reverse is sublime. Napoleon appears in an impossible helmet, crowned with a snake and cluttered with every possible reference to him – the star, the eagle, and the winged thunderbolt.

Two contrasting medals were struck for the Battle of Austerlitz on 2 December 1805, Napoleon's military masterpiece. The first, with the heads of the Emperors Alexander I and Francis II facing, and Napoleon himself on the obverse, is appropriate since the troops are said to have called the battle 'the Battle of the Three Emperors'. The likenesses, however, are not particularly good, perhaps done from portraits. For better likenesses, compare these with those done when the two emperors were actually in Paris in 1814. Napoleon, though he himself is said to have proposed the design, rejected it when shown a proof by Denon and ordered instead the Emperor (some say Charlemagne) enthroned on a winged thunderbolt (Br. 445) – certainly more appropriate for the battle which Napoleon promised to end with 'a thunderclap which shall confound the pride of our enemies!'[7]

AUSTERLITZ AND AFTERMATH

The meeting of Napoleon and the Emperor Francis at Urshutz, two days after the battle on 4 December, was also judged to be worthy of both a painting and a medal.[8] As Francis approached the French Emperor's bivouac, Napoleon said, 'I receive you in the only palace that I have lived in for the last two months.' Francis replied, 'You have turned this habitation to so good an account that it ought to please you.' The meeting took place at two in the afternoon and lasted two hours. An armistice was signed two days later on 6 December.

The medal shows both emperors in ancient dress, that of Napoleon more clearly Roman military. Francis, with one hand on his heart, extends the other

BATTLE OF AUSTERLITZ
(1805). On 2 December 1805, Napoleon defeated the Austrian and Russian armies in his most famous victory, which the soldiers called 'the Day of the Three Emperors'. Napoleon is reported to have suggested the design of this medal to Denon but later to have rejected it, suggesting instead the winged thunderbolt. (Andrieu; Br. 446)

THE EMPEROR FRANCIS VISITS THE MINT
(1814). Francis I of Austria was also in Paris in the spring of 1814, as one of the victors. He visited museums, saw the sights of Paris and had his portrait done by Gayrard. In the museum he admired the models in the ruins of Pola and Spoleto and asked for a catalogue. (Gayrard; Br. 1465)

119

NAPOLEON'S MEDALS: *'Victory to the Arts'*

MEETING AT URSHUTZ (4 December 1805). Two days after Austerlitz at two o'clock in the afternoon the Emperor Francis came to ask for an armistice. An armistice was signed two days later and the Treaty of Pressburg followed on 26 December. This moment was also the subject of a painting. (Chaudet; Andrieu; Br. 452)

TEMPLE OF JANUS IN THE ROMAN FORUM. *Sestertius* of the Emperor Nero (54–68). The Temple with the door closed signifies an Empire at peace.

to Napoleon who offers his right hand with the other on his sword. Between them is the French eagle standard. On the ground are two colours, crossed. The painting by Gross differs primarily in that the figures are in modern dress and there is a third figure, an attendant to Francis.

An imperial decree of 3 March approved Denon's proposal of eighteen paintings, eleven of which have to do with the Austerlitz campaign, among them the 'Address on the Lech Bridge' and the 'Meeting at Urschutz'.[9]

On 13 December the Mayors of Paris visited Napoleon at Schoenbrunn.[10] Their visit was memorialised in a beautiful 68mm medal, conceived by Visconti, drawn by Lamont, and engraved by Brenet (Br. 453). The story of the creation of this medal, one of only two ever struck from hundreds drawn for the Commission by Lamot and others, throws light on the potentialities and the frustrations of the *Commission des inscriptions et Médailles* of the French Academy. Furthermore, the Commission decided this medal did not fit the scheme of their *Histoire métallique,* so another was substituted in their book of drawings (the Battle of Jena; Br. 53). This episode illustrates the years of wasted talent that is the story of the Commission.

The medal for the Peace of Pressburg (Br. 455), 26 December 1805, which ended the war with Austria, shows an elaborate interpretation of the Temple of Janus in the Roman Forum, familiar from the bronze of Nero. The door of the Temple is closed, a sign to France, as to ancient Rome, that the Empire was at peace everywhere. Napoleon was aware of the significance of the Temple of Janus. In a letter to Cambaceres he proposed the building of a Temple of Janus on Montmarte where would be made the 'first solemn proclamations of peace and the distribution of decennial prizes.'[11]

A *Te Deum* was ordered by Napoleon *De Graces Pour la Paix.* It was sung in St Stephen's Cathedral on 28 December 1805, two days after

AUSTERLITZ AND AFTERMATH

the signing of the Peace of Pressburg. A number of the resulting French territorial acquisitions and Austrian losses were celebrated by medals. The takeover of Istria and Dalmatia were commemorated with representations of ancient architectural remains in those countries, the Temple of Augustus at Pola or Istria, the Temple of Jupiter at Split, part of Diocletian's enormous palace, for Dalmatia. The source for these engravings may have been the models in the Paris museum that the Emperor Francis saw and admired on his tour of the city in April 1814.[12]

The return of Venice to Italy, of which Napoleon was now king, was celebrated by Brenet's beautiful medal showing the Rialto Bridge over the Grand Canal (Br. 460). Massena's capture of Naples in February 1806 was commemorated by the use of the familiar Neapolitan coin type, the man-headed bull crowned by Victory. To the ancient symbol Denon has added, beneath the bull's belly, the head of Vulcan, god of the fiery forge. This is clearly a reference to the destruction of Pompeii and Herculaneum by the eruption of Vesuvius in AD 79. Denon the antiquarian, who had spent many years at Naples, would certainly have been aware of that volcanic disaster.

TE DEUM SUNG IN ST STEPHEN'S CATHEDRAL on 28 December, ordered by Napoleon *DE GRACES POUR LA PAIX,* in gratitude for the Peace of Pressburg signed two days earlier, that formalised Austria's humiliation after Austerlitz. (Leperre; Andrieu; Br. 461)

ISTRIA CONQUERED (1806). The Temple of Augustus at Pola in Istria. Ceded to France by the Treaty of Pressburg, 26 December 1805. This temple and the palace of Diocletian were probably copied from models. (Leperre; Brenet; Br. 512)

DALMATIA CONQUERED (1806). Temple of Jupiter at Split. Part of the Emperor Diocletian's enormous palace. Ceded to France by the Treaty of Pressburg. (Leperre; Brenet; Br. 513)

AUSTERLITZ AND AFTERMATH

It is surprising to find Captain Laskey, usually much better informed, mistaking the head of Vulcan under the belly of the bull as 'probably designed for Socrates, emblematic of wisdom, as that animal is of strength.'[13] Scargill's commentary has the correct attribution, as we should expect if the author is really Denon, since Denon spent many years in Naples.

Napoleon had earlier, in June 1805, extended his acquisitions in Italy with the annexation of the Ligurian Republic, the principal city of which was Genoa. On a medal, Napoleon welcomes Liguria into the French Empire. A ship's prow in the background suggests his most important reason for the addition of Genoa, affirmed in a letter to Lebrun on 11 August 1805. He was not after Genoese ships but rather he 'had only one goal, to have 15,000 more sailors.'[14]

With the humiliation of Austria after Austerlitz, the securing of Italy, and his dominant position on the continent, Napoleon was now free to distribute crowns to relatives and loyal generals, as another medal illustrates. To know exactly which sovereignties are intended by the crowns on the table is difficult, but there is general agreement that the two crowns on the floor represent the deposed Kings of Sardinia and Naples and that the cap represents the end of the

VENICE RETURNED TO ITALY (1805). View of the Rialto Bridge over the Grand Canal. Venice was returned to Italy by the terms of the Treaty of Pressburg. Napoleon was now King of Italy. (Leperre; Brenet; Br. 460)

SILVER *NOMOS* OF NEAPOLIS, fourth century BC. Victory flying, crowning a man-headed bull, symbol of the ancient Greek city.

CONQUEST OF NAPLES (1806). Victory flying crowning a man-headed bull, copied from the coin of Neapolis. Denon added a head of Vulcan beneath the belly of the bull, presumably a reference to Vesuvius nearby. The Treaty of Pressburg facilitated the entry of the French Army into Naples on 15 February 1806, and the installation of Joseph Bonaparte as King on 30 March. (Brenet; Br. 516)

AUSTERLITZ AND AFTERMATH

power of the Doge of Venice. As for the crowns on the table, one can only report the new sovereignties created as a result of the destruction of Austrian power and Napoleon's new superiority on the continent.

Bavaria and Wurtemberg became kingdoms and the Margravete of Baden a Duchy by the Treaty of Pressburg. On 16 February Napoleon adopted Josephine's son, Eugene, and made him heir to the Kingdom of Italy. In March he adopted Stephanie, Josephine's niece, and married her to the Prince of Baden and created Murat Duke of Berg and Cleves. At the end of March he made his brother Joseph King of Naples. Pauline Borghese became Princess and Duchess of Guastalla, brother Lewis, King of Holland, Marshal Berthier, Prince of Neufchtel, Talleyrand, Prince of Benevento and Marshal Bernadotte, Prince of Ponte-Corvo.

LIGURIA UNITED TO FRANCE (1805). Napoleon welcomes the city of Genoa while the Imperial Eagle looks on. Even before Austerlitz, Genoa, the principal city of the Ligurian Republic, had yielded to French pressure to join the Empire. Austerlitz confirmed French dominion in Italy. What Napoleon wanted primarily was Genoese sailors. Actually struck in 1809. (Fragonard; Brenet; Br. 422)

SOVEREIGNTIES GIVEN (1806). A table with crowns and sceptres before the imperial throne; three broken crowns lie on the floor. An eagle above holds the *fasces*, Roman symbol of authority. A sceptre laid across the throne has an effigy of Napoleon. The victories of 1805, the Treaty of Pressburg, and new alliances made kingdoms available to Napoleon for his relatives. The three broken crowns may refer to the expulsion of the Kings of Naples and Sardinia and the destruction of the power of the Doge of Venice. (Zix; Andrieu; Br. 553)

125

Notes

1. Ernest Babelon, *Médailles Historiques de Régne de Napoléon le Grand,* Paris, 1912, p.xx, xxi. The medal was done several months after the visit. The visit itself, with the speeches of the Mayors and Napoleon's reply, is recorded in *Le Moniteur* for 25 December 1805.
2. Griffiths, *The Medal,* 17 (1990), 37ff.
3. Fifth Bulletin of the Grand Army, *Le Moniteur,* 18 October 1805.
4. A letter in the Paris archive quoted by Lelièvre.
5. *Le Moniteur,* Nov. 26, 1805.
6. *Napoleonic Medals* VII, p.6.
7. Thirteenth Bulletin of the Grand Army, *Le Moniteur,* 16 December 1805.
8. The 31st Bulletin of the Grand Army has Saruschitz, but the medal reads Urshitz (Urschutz).
9. Pierre Lelièvre, *Vivant Denon, Directeur des Beaux-Artes de Napoléon.* Paris: Libraire Floury, p.60. pp.67ff. gives a detailed account of the choice of painting subjects and artists for this and later campaigns, and indicative of the relation between Denon and the Emperor for the production of medals, from correspondence in the French archives. It is interesting that Gross (in this proposal) was to receive 12,000 francs for the painting, and Andrieu, the engraver of the medal, 1800 francs. Chaudet (the famous sculptor) as artist would receive 800 francs.
10. Thirty-sixth Bulletin of the Grand Army, *Le Moniteur,* 25 December 1805.
11. Corresp. 14510. 26 November 1808.
12. *Le Moniteur,* 28 April 1814.
13. p.116.
14. Corresp. 9064.

XII

Prussia

A series of marriage alliances, which contributed to Napoleon's confederation of the Rhine, were more significant for the future of the Empire than any military moves. On 3 March the hereditary Prince of Baden arrived and had dinner with the Emperor and Empress.[1] On the next day Napoleon reported to the Senate the adoption of Josephine's niece, Stephanie, and her betrothal to the Prince.[2] He declared that 'the distinguished qualities of Prince Charles of Baden and the particular affection which he has shown to us in all circumstances are a sure guarantee of the happiness of our daughter.' Finally, the Emperor called attention to 'an alliance which is very agreeable to us'. The wedding took place at Paris on 8 April, with celebration suited to the occasion.[3] All the officers of state were there and foreign dignitaries, and the Emperor himself gave the bride away.

A charming medal by Andrieu celebrates the marriage. The Prince and Princess are seen as the meeting of Jacob and Rachel, clasping hands in a tender moment. The true meaning of the event, however, is clear from the medal. In bold letters in the exergue may be read *ALLIANCE*, and the tender scene is illuminated by a radiant 'N' above, reflecting that telling closing phrase of Napoleon's speech to the Senate, 'an alliance which is very agreeable to us'. Napoleon's hegemony in Germany is clearly more important to him than the future happiness of the couple.

MARRIAGE OF THE PRINCE OF BADEN (1806). Sensitive scene of the meeting of Jacob and Rachel symbolises the marriage of the Prince of Baden to Bonaparte's niece Stephanie, one of Napoleon's alliances in support of the Confederation of the Rhine. The inscription in the exergue (*ALLIANCE*) and the radiant 'N' above make it clear that Napoleon's German hegemony rather than the future of the happy couple is contemplated. (Andrieu; Br. 522)

NAPOLEON'S MEDALS: *'Victory to the Arts'*

ALLIANCE WITH SAXONY (1806). The Emperors Napoleon and Charlemagne. On the reverse (above) are Wittikind, the ancient Saxon king, and Frederick Augustus, the current sovereign. Frederick, formerly Elector of Saxony, was made king of an expanded kingdom when he joined Napoleon's alliance. Napoleon himself made the parallel with Charlemagne explicit. 'I am Charlemagne, for like Charlemagne I have united the crowns of France and Lombardy,' he wrote in 1806. (Bergeret; Andrieu; Br. 551)

One should not be surprised by the strict control of the royal marriage, even without the imperial decree published in *Le Moniteur* on 1 April providing for imperial oversight of all phases of activity of members of the royal family, specifically including marriage. This adds spice to the emperor's rage at hearing of the marriage of Jérôme, Napoleon's younger brother, to Miss Patterson of Baltimore, which Napoleon promptly declared annulled.

On 11 December 1806 Elector Frederick Augustus of Saxony became King of Saxony and joined his new kingdom to Napoleon's Confederation of the Rhine. The medal produced in honour of the new alliance shows the two Emperors, Napoleon and Charlemagne, on one side and Wittikind and Frederick Augustus on the other. Napoleon was arguing an historic parallel: just as Charlemagne, centuries earlier had recognised Wittikind as King of Saxony, so Napoleon had made Frederick Augustus king of the same country.

Napoleon had already seen himself as the heir of Charlemagne, as his coronation as King of Italy in Milan with the crown of Agilulfus, King of the Lombards shows, in the tradition of Charlemagne who had made himself King of the Lombards. Napoleon crowned himself, remembering Pope Leo and Charlemagne.

King Friedrich of Prussia correctly perceived these political moves of Napoleon as a threat to his country. But his declaration of war was ill conceived. It was followed by the disastrous defeat at Jena on 14 October 1806 and Napoleon's occupation of Berlin on the 26th. Of the two medals struck, Bergeret's vision of Napoleon on Jupiter's eagle is superior to that of the Commission, Napoleon riding over fallen soldiers, the only medal ever struck of the hundreds conceived and drawn for their book to be presented to the Emperor. The *quadriga* on top of the Brandenburg Gate was taken to Paris where the Prussians found it in April 1814, being restored.

PRUSSIA

Napoleon was not merely *like* Charlemagne – he *was* Charlemagne – at least in his own eyes. Upset that the Pope did not understand history, he wrote to his uncle, Cardinal Fesch.[4]

> As far as the Pope is concerned, I am Charlemagne, for like Charlemagne I have united the crowns of France and Lombardy, and my Empire extends to the borders of the Orient ... If he behaves well I will change nothing. Otherwise I will reduce the Pope to be the Bishop of Rome.

Also commemorating the victories of 1806 is the splendid medallion of Napoleon as Hercules (Br. 554, p.40) wearing his lion skin, with club and Jupiter's thunderbolt in the field. On the reverse, enclosed in a wreath, is a list of the principal conquests of that year, *ISTRIE, DALMATIE, NAPLES, IENA, BERLIN*. Two grand monuments copied from antiquity – the Column of the *Place Vendôme*, derived from Trajan's column for the Dacian War, and the Carrousel Arch, a version of the Arch of Septimius Severus in the Roman Forum – were dedicated to victorious French armies. These are also displayed on medals of 1806.

One of the most beautiful French river medals celebrates his arrival at the Vistula late in 1806. The nymph of the river hangs her head at the sight of the French eagle.

The campaigns of 1807, with Russia the primary antagonist, were more difficult, though just as decisive in the end. The year began with the bloody standoff at Eylau, fought with the Russians in a snowstorm on 7 February, after which both armies

BATTLE OF JENA

Napoleon gallops over Prussian soldiers below. The only medal of the Commission of Inscriptions and Medals, of the Class of History and Ancient Literature that was struck by the *Monnaie des Médailles*. (Andrieu; Br. 537)

NAPOLEON AS JUPITER. Battle of Jena. Riding his eagle, he rains thunderbolts on the giants below, destroying the Prussian Army. (Bergeret; Galle; Br. 538)

ENTRY INTO BERLIN The Brandenburg Gate (1806). After shattering the Prussian Army at Jena and Aurstadt, Napoleon entered Berlin on 26 October 1806. On 21 November he issued the Berlin Decree, announcing the complete blockade of England. The *quadriga* on top of the Brandenburg Gate was taken to Paris where it was undergoing restoration when reclaimed by the King of Prussia in April 1814 – but not before a cast was made of one of the horses for the equestrian statue of Henry IV. (Leperre; Jaley: Br 546)

retreated to winter quarters. Napoleon chose to portray the battle as a victory, reporting 1,900 casualties, and 12–15,000 Russian prisoners,[5] whereas the number of dead on each side was probably about the same, approximately 18,000.

Napoleon's claim of victory was technically true because he held the field of battle after the Russians withdrew. But Marshal Ney's assessment was 'What a slaughter, and what did we achieve? Nothing.'[6] This was closer to the truth. He wrote to Josephine on 14 February. 'My Dear, I am still at Eylau. This ground is covered with dead and wounded. That is not the beautiful part of war …'

That truth may have given rise to this comment by Denon in *Le Moniteur*.[7]

> The Battle of Eylau is one of those events which occupy in history a singular place … in particular for the painter, who alone can render the harshness of the site and of the climate and the severity of the season in which that memorable battle has taken place.

There follows a direction to the competition for the painting that it should be of the moment after the battle when the Emperor visits the battlefield. The result is the masterpiece by Gross, which shows Napoleon with his fellow marshals touring the battlefield, but only Napoleon seems genuinely concerned about the death around him.

Denon is certainly correct. The painting more than the medal can show the horror of the battlefield and the nuances of the feeling of the Emperor. Yet the medal in this case has its place. It shows Napoleon as Diomedes, the friend of Ulysses, seated on top of a pile of arms with victory in one hand and drawn sword in the other. *VICTORIAE MANENTI* – 'to constant victory'). The victory remains but the drawn sword shows that the war it not over.

Having retired to winter quarters at Osterode, Napoleon did not attempt to engage the enemy again until June. This long hiatus in military activity is explained in a curious way, by a medal with one of the few ancient military figures to appear on Napoleon's medals (Br. 631). *FABIUS CUNCTATOR*, 'Fabius the Delayer' is not the hero one would expect Bonaparte – the master of rapid military movement – to choose. However un-Napoleonic, Andrieu's portrait is inspired. No ancient representations of Fabius have survived, but the artist has caught the spirit of the stubborn old soldier who defied both Hannibal and Roman public opinion to save his country. The point is clear, as Fabius would not fight Hannibal when victory was uncertain, Napoleon refused to fight the enemy until he was ready.

The British also had their *FABIUS CUNCTATOR*, Wellington pausing behind the lines of Torres Vedras in 1810–11. Napoleon's strategy was justified in the event, at the Battle of Friedland on 14 June 1807. The medal for that victory shows Napoleon as Mars, sheathing his sword on the battlefield; the torch of war is finally extinguished. Napoleon took notice of the fact that Friedland was fought on the same day as Marengo. A medal has Victory writing the two battles on a shield beneath the date.

BATTLE OF EYLAU (1807). Napoleon as Diomedes, bold warrior companion of Odysseus at Troy, sits on a pile of arms with Victory in one hand and a drawn sword in the other. The victory was bloody and indecisive. The war, Napoleon knew, was not over. Diomedes must fight again. (Brenet; Br 628)

NAPOLEON AT OSTERODE (1807). An inspired representation of the stubborn old Roman, 'Fabius the Delayer'. Napoleon justifies his long stay at Osterode after the difficult Battle of Eylau (8 February 1807). Fabius' refusal to fight Hannibal was the right decision. Napoleon's delay was justified by the decisive victory of Friedland (14 June 1807). (Andrieu; Br. 631)

132

PRUSSIA

A medal for the conquest of Silesia is a summary of the reduction of several fortresses of that area over a period of time. A tower of crowns lists the cities captured. Victory is writing the names of the fortresses on a shield. Peace behind restrains her. One city remains unconquered, its crown on the ground – *SILBERBERG*.

WELLINGTON AS *FABIUS CUNCTATOR*
Wellington depicted as a Roman general, waiting on the lines of the Torres Vedras until he was ready. Seen as 'Fabius the Delayer', as was Napoleon at Osterode. In both cases the delay was justified by the result. (Mudie, 1820. Petit and Dubois; Br. 1138)

NAPOLEON'S MEDALS: *Victory to the Arts*

BATTLE OF FRIEDLAND

(1807). Napoleon as Mars sheaths his sword amidst the carnage of battle. The torch of war is extinguished. An olive branch signifies peace. (Chaudet; Br. 632)

VICTORY INSCRIBES A SHIELD AT FRIEDLAND

(1807). Victory inscribes a shield with the victories won on the same day, 14 June – Marengo and Friedland. (Brenet; Br. 633)

For the Peace of Tilsit that sealed the victory, Napoleon had constructed an elaborate pavilion which he anchored in the centre of the River Nieman. The medal for Tilsit has the river god holding aloft a model of the pavilion, an oak tree, representing peace, growing at his feet. The obverse shows the three sovereigns, Napoleon and Alexander crowned but Friedrich Wilhelm without any adornment.

PRUSSIA

The Peace of Tilsit was negotiated in the pavilion on 21 June, Napoleon and Alexander alone. Another medal shows the two emperors embracing while Friedrich waits on the shore, hat in hand (Br. 641). The next day Friedrich was included but Napoleon was rude to him as he intended, but charmed Alexander, and was charmed by him.

Napoleon wrote to Josephine, 'My dear, I have just come from seeing the Emperor Alexander; I am very content with him; he is very good looking, a good and young emperor; he has more spirit than is commonly thought.' Herold, from an unofficial source adds the words, 'and he must be satisfied with me. If he were a woman I think I would make him my mistress.'[8]

For Jérôme, who by several military actions had regained the Emperor's favour, Napoleon created the Kingdom of Westphalia. Jérôme became king on 18 August 1807 and on the 22nd married Princess Catherine. Napoleon was impressed with the Princess. In a letter to General Savary: 'We have celebrated at Paris the marriage of the King of Westphalia … I should not fail to speak to you about the Princess: She is very beautiful, with a very fine figure …'[9]

CONQUEST OF SILESIA (1807). Victory writes on a shield. Peace behind restrains her hand. Seven mural crowns form a column naming seven Silesian cities captured, to complete the conquest of this Prussian territory. A crown on the ground names one city spared through Napoleon's forbearance. (Meynier; Andrieu; Br. 635)

THE THREE SOVEREIGNS AT TILSIT (July 1807). The three sovereigns, Napoleon, Alexander I of Russia and Frederick William III of Prussia. Napoleon and Alexander are laureate; Frederick is uncrowned. Napoleon's view and the true state of affairs at Tilsit; Frederick did not count. (Andrieu; Br. 640)

PEACE OF TILSIT – THE NIEMEN (July 1807). The god of the river, reclining on his urn, holds aloft the raft-pavilion where the two Emperors met. Frederick had no part in the negotiations. (Meynier; Droz; Br. 640)

136

PRUSSIA

On the medal itself, celebrating the creation of the Kingdom, a young man, laurel-crowned, is in the act of staying a horse at full gallop. The inscription reads, 'At length he bridles in its wandering course'. Generally thought to be a copy of the Alexander and Bucephalus at Rome, the theme may be another reference to Hanover, incorporated into Westphalia, as 'a land of fine horses'. A wedding medal for this occasion, drawn by the great painter, Prudhon, and engraved by Andrieu, is a charming scene in which Hymen makes a garland of roses given to him by Cupid.

CREATION OF THE KINGDOM OF WESTPHALIA. 'At length he bridles in its wandering course.' A young man, laurel crowned, in the act of staying a horse in full gallop. Generally thought to be a representation of Alexander and Bucephalus in Rome. It may also represent Hanover incorporated into the Kingdom of Westphalia by Napoleon. (Brenet; Br. 660)

NAPOLEON'S MEDALS: *'Victory to the Arts'*

MARRIAGE OF JÉRÔME NAPOLEON, King of Westphalia, to Catherine of Wurtemburg (22 August 1807). Hymen makes a garland of roses given him by Cupid. This was part of Napoleon's (ultimately failed) system of alliances. (Prudhon; Andrieu; Br. 662).

CAMPAIGNS OF 1806–1807 – THREE CAPITALS (1807). Three turreted women, each with keys to her city. Berlin was entered in October 1806, Warsaw in November 1806 and Königsberg in June 1807. Summary of the war with Russia on Prussian soil. (George; Br. 634)

Jérôme's career as King of Westphalia was much less impressive. Napoleon's letters to the new monarch spell out his sins in detail. The most severe of these were not included in the official collection. On 16 July 1808, the Emperor wrote

> You owe the bank two millions. You allow your notes to be repudiated … There must be an end to the mad extravagance which already makes you the laughing stock of Europe, and will end by rousing the indignation of your subjects …[10]

Jérôme is the best example of the problems inherent in Napoleon's attempt to rule Europe through his family.

A summary medal for the campaigns of 1806–1807 shows three maidens, each named for her city and carrying a key – Berlin, Warsaw, Konigsberg – standing for Napoleon's triumph over those Prussian cities.

Notes

1. *Le Moniteur*, 4 March 1806.
2. Corresp. 9923.
3. *Le Moniteur*, 10 April 1806.
4. Corresp. 9656.
5. Corresp. 11791.
6. Eric Perrin, *Le Maréchal Ney*, p.106. Cited in Schom, *Napoleon Bonaparte*, p.828, n. 14.
7. *Le Moniteur*, 2 April 1807.
8. J. Christopher Herold, *The Age of Napoleon*, p.184.
9. Corresp. 13073.
10. Thompson, *Napoleon's Letters*, No, 164.

XIII

Austria

PEACE OF PRESSBURG (1805). The Temple of Janus, with the door closed, copied from the coin of Nero, with some architectural elaboration. Peace signed with Austria after Austerlitz, December 1805. (Leperre; Andrieu; Br. 455)

With Europe pacified, there were few historical events worthy of a medal in the year 1808[1] other than the rare victory from the otherwise ill-starred Spanish Campaign. In April 1809, however, the Austrians invaded Bavaria and Italy, breaking the Peace of Pressburg signed at the end of 1805. Napoleon's artists used the Temple of Janus motif creatively to show the making and breaking of the treaty. As the medal for the Peace of Pressburg showed the doors of the Temple of Janus with the doors closed, (see p.120 for this scene on a *sestertius* of the Emperor Nero) so the breaking of the peace shows the doors fractured, the pieces lying on the steps.

AUSTRIA

The Austrian move, sooner than expected (9 April 1809), caught the French unprepared and poorly positioned. Just in time (22 April), Napoleon launched a flank attack that sent the Austrian Army retreating northward. The victory is remembered on a medal which shows Napoleon in Roman military dress before two trophies of enemy arms (Br. 844). The next day Napoleon in a difficult battle took the Fortress city of Ratisbon, an event remembered in Manfredini's creative use of the Battle of Gods and Giants myth. A giant (perhaps the Austrian Archduke Charles) is shown buried under Mount Aetna (or Sicily, or Kos, according to the version one accepts); the mountain was thrown by Minerva (or Jupiter). The inscription may stand for the whole series of battles that began with the Austrian presumption in attacking Napoleon: *AGGRESSUS MAGNUM RESCINDERE COELUM* ('He tried to scale the heights of heaven'), and the divine punishment, *AUSTRIACIS FULMINE DEIECTIS* ('The Austrians destroyed by thunderbolts').

The way was now open to Vienna. Napoleon advertised the speed of his advance with a medal. He left St Martin's Gate in Paris on 13 April 1809 and entered Vienna by the Carinthie Gate on 13 May, exactly one month later. But the crossing of the Danube to confront the Austrian Army still lay before him. An attempt at Essling in May 1809 resulted in one of Napoleon's rare defeats (Br 859). When the

TREATY OF PRESSBURG BROKEN BY AUSTRIA (1809). The violence of the act is suggested by the broken door, the pieces of which lie on the steps. Austria attacked Napoleon's German Confederation in April of 1809, taking the French by surprise. (Andrieu; Br. 844)

ABENSBERG AND ECKMUHL (1809). Napoleon in Roman military dress between two trophies of arms. Austria's decision early in 1809 to attack Napoleon's German Confederation, breaking the Peace of Pressburg, caught Napoleon off guard and his advance force scattered. He saved the situation by brilliant manoeuvring at the Battles of Abensberg and Eckmuhl (20 and 22 April 1809). (Bergeret; Brenet; Br. 844)

BATTLE OF RATISBON (1809). A giant (according to one view, the Archduke Charles, the Austrian commander) buried under Mount Aetna. The inscription focuses on the daring of the Austrian attack, 'He tried to scale the heights of heaven' and its complete failure, 'The Austrians destroyed by thunderbolts'. (Manfredini; Br. 846)

142

AUSTRIA

Emperor threw a pontoon bridge across the rain-swollen Danube, the angry god of that river, *DANUBIUS PONTEM INDIGNATUS*, broke up the bridge causing considerable loss of life. Napoleon had to withdraw.

Daru, whom Napoleon had designated to approve the medals presented to him, had some carping criticism.[2] He thought the medal too difficult to explain and insisted that Napoleon prefered inscriptions to be in French. Denon explained the medal succinctly and ignored the linguistic objection. The appropriate Latin phrase appeared on the medal.

A successful crossing downstream six weeks later pictured on the reverse of the medal, made possible the decisive victory at Wagram. In this battle Hercules rescuing Victory (Br. 860) or Victory hurling a thunderbolt (Br. 862) came to Napoleon's aid. Meanwhile, Prince Eugene had driven another Austrian army beyond the Raab, pictured as a river god leaning on his urn, while behind him peasants flee to the mountains (Br. 854). The medal Br. 847 shows the speed with which Napoleon's army negotiated the distance between Paris and Vienna by depicting the gates of the cities.

A final medallic comment on the Campaign of 1809 concerns the British attack on Antwerp while Napoleon was still at Schoenbrunn. The city is shown standing with grounded spear and foot on the prow of a ship. Napoleon remained at Schoenbrunn; Jupiter would take care of the British – as indeed he did! The city's natural defences and the unhealthy climate were more than a match for the British Army. There are long accounts in *Le Moniteur*, quoting the British press, about first the health of the troops and then the official enquiry as to what went wrong.

ENTRY INTO VIENNA

St Martin's Gate, Paris; Carinthie Gate, Vienna. Napoleon left Paris on 13 April and entered Vienna on 13 May, moving the Army at great speed. (Andrieu; Br. 847)

143

NAPOLEON'S MEDALS: *Victory to the Arts*

◀ **ENGLISH ATTACK ON ANTWERP** (1809). Goddess of the city with caduceus and grounded spear. Neither the goddess or Napoleon – who remained at Schoenbrunn – were disturbed by the English attack in July 1809. On the obverse of this medal, JUPITER STATOR, who stopped the attack of Rome's enemies and would do the same to the English. Disease decimated the English force. (Lafitte; Depaulis; Br. 870)

PEACE OF VIENNA (1809). Napoleon, laurel crowned, places an olive branch on an altar with his right hand while with his left torching a pile of military debris (mortars and cannon). The treaty signed on 14 October 1809 ended the war with Austria. (Lafitte; Andrieu; Br. 876) ▶

Napoleon's artists saw this in terms of a story in Livy,[3] where Romulus fleeing from the Sabines prayed to 'Jupiter Stator' (Jupiter, Stayer of Flight), so that the Romans turned and defeated their enemies. The obverse of the medal (Br. 870) therefore shows JUPITER STATOR, a splendid representation of the King of the Gods.

The Peace of Vienna that formally ended the conflict is commemorated on a medal in which Napoleon places an olive branch on an altar with one hand while torching an assembly of cannon and armaments with the other. When Daru protested that the iron of cannon and howitzers would not burn, Denon replied that he would substitute armaments of which the wooden supports would prove flammable (Br. 876).[4]

The climax of the long history of conflict with the papacy was the Pope's arrest at his palace on the Quirinal on 6 July 1809. But Napoleon already had the Papal

ROME AND PARIS (1809). Two ladies with elaborate headdress – a ship for Paris and a wolf with twins for Rome. The Roman states were incorporated into the Empire by a decree issued in Vienna, 17 May 1809. For the same event the god of the Tiber watches the French Eagle return to its home on the Capitol. (Lafitte; Depaulis; Br. 849)

VISIT OF THE KING AND QUEEN OF BAVARIA TO THE MEDAL MINT (1810). Maximillian Joseph, Napoleon's most faithful ally – he had to be to prevent Austria from taking territory from Bavaria. Andrieu's realistic portrait reveals the strain of the King's not entirely successful effort to hold his diverse country together. The sovereigns' visit to Paris came immediately after Napoleon's Second Austrian Campaign and immediately before Napoleon's marriage to the Austrian Princess Marie Louise on 1 April 1810. The King and Queen did *not* come to Paris for the wedding. They went home to Bavaria more than a month before it took place. Maximillian was opposed to the match since it meant a closer alliance between France and Bavaria's natural enemy, Austria. (Andrieu; Br. 939)

145

States. A decree issued at Vienna, 17 May 1809, incorporated the Roman states into the French Empire. The medal celebrating this shows two ladies (Rome and Paris), with elaborate hairdos, a ship for Paris and wolf and twins for Rome, symbolising the French possession of the Papal States including Rome. The same event is seen as the god of the Tiber (Br. 848) watching the French eagle carrying a thunderbolt to his temple on the Capitol. A wolf, with only one twin, watches at the side.

Among those who came to Paris to congratulate Napoleon on his victory were the King and Queen of Bavaria. It so happened that Napoleon was in the midst of marriage negotiations. They did not stay for the wedding. Maximillian, King of Bavaria, was naturally opposed to an alliance that drew France and Austria – Bavaria's natural enemy – closer together.

The portrait by Andrieu of the Bavarian sovereigns is masterful. Maximillian Joseph, Napoleon's most faithful ally, shows the strain of his not entirely successful effort to hold his country together and the Queen's firm mouth is in line with her character.

The remainder of Napoleon's history, recorded on the medals, belongs to the reversal of fortune, beginning with the Russian Campaign.

Notes

1　For the background see Rose, *Life of Napoleon I,* II, p.180ff.
2　24 January 1811, Antony Griffiths, *The design and production of Napoleon's Histoire Métallique,* Appendix 2, p.28.
3　I, 12.
4　Griffiths, loc cit.

XIV

The Face of History

Images of Bonaparte

The medallic portraits of Napoleon Bonaparte are in the most literal sense, 'The Face of History'. The images of Bonaparte, before the portrait became standardised at the beginning of the Empire with the images of Andrieu and Droz inspired by the statue of Chaudet, are fascinating in their variety. This variety is the result of many different factors – the development of hairstyle, shifts from realism to idealism, differences in artistic view, and of course the political need to project an inspiring vision. On one or two occasions there is a reflection of imperial figures in the past.

The earliest portrait of Bonaparte connected with the First Italian Campaign appears to be a true likeness. In particular, the nose is large. The long hair, the style of the time, appears also in paintings of Bonaparte from this period. There is no idealisation in this medal addressed to 'Buonaparte, General in Chief of the brave army of Italy' and declaring 'Your soldiers will enjoy the fruit of their labours'.

◄ **BUONAPARTE, GENERAL IN CHIEF OF THE BRAVE ITALIAN ARMY** (1796). One of the earliest medals struck in Bonaparte's honour. (H. 767), 32mm.

◄ **REVERSE OF H. 767.** Minerva holding an olive branch, leaning on a fasces and sitting on a pile of arms and flags. The inscription reads 'BEHOLD VALOROUS SOLDIERS THE FRUIT OF YOUR LABOURS.'

GAYRARD – BATTLE OF MONTENOTTE
Idealised and archaising portrait of Bonaparte with long hair. The battle was fought in 1796 but the medal was not struck until 1813.
(Gayrard; H. 731)

DUVIVIER – GENERAL BONAPARTE (1798). Early realistic portrait from the period of the First Italian Campaign.
(Duvivier; H. 811), 56mm.

THE FACE OF HISTORY

The medals for 'The Five Battles', which Napoleon ordered at Milan and assigned to Appiani to draw and to Lavy to engrave, have no portraits, since to place the General's effigy on an official medal was considered too bold a move. The portrait on the medal for the Battle of Montenotte is an idealised portrait with long hair in the style of the time but was not produced until 1813, and has Bonaparte's features smoothed out.

There are several medals for the Peace of Campoformio that ended the First Italian Campaign. The Italicus medal, by a tobacco merchant at Strasbourg (H. 812), has been discussed above. The most striking of these medals was done at Lyons by Chauvanne (H. 816), for the citizens and merchants of the city. An inscription in the exergue of the reverse claims that he 'does not fight except for peace and the rights of man'. The familiar ring of these revolutionary words shows how thoroughly Lyons was immersed in the ideals of the Revolution at that time. Three years later, as we have seen, Bonaparte visited the city and did the citizens the honour of laying the first stone in the rebuilding after the destruction in a war with the French government. The bust, also done by Chauvanne (Br. 59), resembles the former piece but has curly and somewhat shorter hair.

The large medal for the Peace of Campoformio by Duvivier (H. 811) has a splendid portrait on the obverse in the realistic style with long hair, but was really done for the arrival in Paris of the Italian treasures in July 1798.

An early (1800) portrait by Lavy has shorter hair that still extends below the ears. A year later, both Droz and Andrieu have portraits with the hair a little shorter, but still not idealised. By 1802, Andrieu's portrait shows him well on the way to the idealisation of the standard portrait based on the statue by Chaudet.

▼ **BUST OF BONAPARTE 'GENERAL IN CHIEF OF THE ARMY OF ITALY'** (1797). Addressed to the General by 'the citizens and artisans of Lyons'. The city was staunchly Bonapartist. In January 1811 Napoleon would forbid the wearing of military dress at court and insist on embroidered silk suits, partly in an attempt to stimulate the manufacturing industry of Lyons at a time of economic crisis. (Chavanne; H. 816)

◄ **REVERSE OF H. 816.** Minerva holding an olive branch and a horn of abundance. In front of the goddess is an altar on which are two hands are joined. The legend below reads 'HE DOES NOT FIGHT BUT FOR PEACE AND RIGHTS OF MAN.'

NAPOLEON'S MEDALS: *'Victory to the Arts'*

Later in the year, on the obverse of 'The Return of Astree', Droz has created another idealisation (Br. 200).

Two medallions of 1803 are a curious variation on the idealised portrait. The obverse of the Venus de Medici medal (Br. 280) strikes one as a possible likeness of Julius Caesar. Another, by Brenet, (Br. 275) is more clearly Augustus, a resemblance noted in Bonaparte's lifetime. A unique variation of the idealised portrait is Joannin's frontal view with a crown of lotus, struck for the Egyptian Campaign but actually published in 1808.

LAVY – THE CISALPINE REPUBLIC RESTORED (1800). (Lavy; Br. 42), 52mm.

DROZ – PEACE OF LUNEVILLE (1801). Bonaparte as seen by another great artist. (Droz; Br. 106)

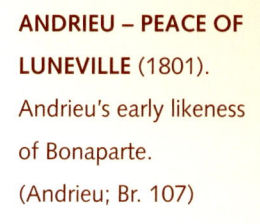

ANDRIEU – PEACE OF LUNEVILLE (1801). Andrieu's early likeness of Bonaparte. (Andrieu; Br. 107)

ANDRIEU – PUBLIC INSTRUCTION (1802). A year later than the previous portrait – more idealised. (Andrieu; Br. 214)

DROZ – PEACE OF AMIENS (1802). Reverse of the Return of Astree. (Droz; Br. 200)

**ANDRIEU
– REESTABLISHMENT
OF RELIGION** (1802).
Another portrayal by the
artist. (Andrieu; Br. 213)

**BRENET
– A *LA FORTUNE
CONSERVATRICE***
(1803). Bonaparte as
Augustus, a resemblance
noted in his lifetime.
(Brenet; Br. 275), 34mm.

JEUFFROY – BONAPARTE AS JULIUS CAESAR? (1803). (Jeuffroy; Br. 280)

JOUANNIN – CONQUEST OF EGYPT (1798). Possibly the only frontal portrait depicted on a medal. He is shown with a crown of lotus instead of laurel. Not struck until 1808. (Jouannin; H. 879)

NAPOLEON'S MEDALS: *'Victory to the Arts'*

ANDRIEU – STANDARD IMPERIAL PORTRAIT
Napoleon as Emperor. Standard portrait for most of the Imperial period. After the statue by Chaudet. (Andrieu; Br. 662).

GALLE – CORONATION FESTIVITIES (1804).
Napoleon as Emperor. (Galle; Br. 358), 68mm.

Imperial Portraits

The idealised Andrieu portrait became the standard obverse type in the Imperial period. Before May 1805, however, when Napoleon crowned himself King of Italy at Milan, several medals omit the attribution *Roi*. The most notable of these is the large (68mm) portrait by Galle that on the reverse celebrated the coronation festivities. Occasional portraits by Droz, Jeuffroy and Brenet endured to the end of the Empire.

Manfredini and his workshop in Italy took a slightly different tack. The earliest of these medals are two from 1805; one is the medal for the coronation in Milan and the other shows Napoleon in a strange helmet, designed to display his honours and attributes. We can recognise the thunderbolt, the laurel crown and the Imperial Eagle. On the visor of the helmet is his star of Destiny.

MANFREDINI – CORONATION IN MILAN (1805). (Manfredini; Br. 420)

MANFREDINI – THE CAPTURE OF VIENNA (1805). Napoleon in a fanciful helmet, designed to display his honours and attributes. We recognise the thunderbolt, laurel crown and the Imperial Eagle. On the visor is his star of destiny. This is the obverse of *Vindobona Capta*. The snake remains unexplained. (Br. 444)

NAPOLEON'S MEDALS: *'Victory to the Arts'*

MANFREDINI – BATTLE OF WAGRAM (1809). Napoleon wearing the Iron Crown as King of Italy with full titles: 'Napoleon the Great, Emperor of the French, King of Italy, Pious, Happy, August, Invincible.' (Br. 862)

One later portrait by Manfredini (1809) has Napoleon wearing the Iron Crown as King of Italy. He has titles outclassing most Roman emperors: 'Napoleon the Great; Emperor of the French; King of Italy; Pious; Happy; August; Invincible.' Another, without a crown (by Vassalo, in Manfredini's workshop), may resemble the Greek god Apollo – but the thunderbolt belongs to Zeus.

One distinctive portrait by Droz survives from the period of the Russian disaster. It does not, however, appear in any of the early Mint lists and in size, 55mm, does not fit the Denon series and lacks his name as Director. The reverse

THE FACE OF HISTORY

is Hercules battling the Giants. It was certainly engraved by Droz but may have been produced later.

By far the grandest portrait of Napoleon is that by Edouard Gatteaux, son of the distinguished late eighteenth century medallist Nicolas Gatteaux. The medal was done at the French Academy in Rome. This medal is of Napoleon enthroned in royal robes, holding a crown in his right hand, cradling a sceptre in his left arm while fingering the hilt of a sword. The inscription dates it to 1812 but the medal was not struck until 1814, when Gatteaux returned to Paris after the first restoration of Louis XVIII. This was the beginning of a long and illustrious career for Gatteaux under the French monarchy.

VASSALO – BATTLE OF RATISBON (from Manfredini's workshop – 1809). We may imagine the Greek god Apollo – but the thunderbolt belongs to Zeus. (Vassalo; Br. 846)

157

◄ **DROZ – HERCULES TIES UP THE NEMEAN LION** (1804). (Droz; Br. 320)

► **DROZ – BATTLE OF MOSCOW** (1812). Obviously by Droz but probably struck some time later. (Droz; Br. 1162), 55mm.

◄ **GATTEAUX – FRENCH SCHOOL OF ARTS IN ROME** (1812). Gatteaux's tribute to the French School of Fine Arts at Rome is the obverse of this medal. Gatteaux's splendid portrait of Napoleon enthroned is dated 1812 but the *Trésor* was not actually produced until May of 1814. Apparently – and strangely – it was struck in Paris on Gatteaux's return to France to take up the office of medallist to Louis XVIII at his First Restoration. (Gatteaux; Br. 1178), 58mm.

158

◄ **BRENET – THE BATTLE OF LÜTZEN** (1813). The military bust appears in 1813. British engravers borrowed this portrait after the war. (Br. 1229)

BRENET – THE SECOND ABDICATION (1815). ►
Compare this with the above. The nobility is gone, as well it might be in a medal recording the final humiliation. (Br. 1664)

◄ **ANDRIEU – DEATH OF NAPOLEON** (1821). With Napoleon's Death Andrieu's idealised portrait is used again. Napoleon's most important victories are inscribed on the wreath encircling the portrait. (Br. 1844), lead, 69mm.

159

NAPOLEON'S MEDALS: *'Victory to the Arts'*

BOVY – NAPOLEON'S REMAINS REMOVED TO PARIS (1840). The hero returns home. (Br. 1990)

The military bust by Brenet appears in 1813 along with the standard portrait but appears less imperial than the Chaudet-inspired image. A further deterioration may be perceived in Brenet's image of Napoleon on the medal recording the Second Abdication.

With the death of Napoleon in 1821, Andrieu returned to the Chaudet-inspired portrait, a 69mm piece in lead. It had the head of Napoleon encircled by a wreath on which were inscribed his principal victories. The return of the hero's remains in 1840 gave Bovy an opportunity for a final portrait, which showed on the reverse his burial site on St Helena.

XV

The Family

The medals of Napoleon can only hint at the two major themes that run through the story of his family – the failed attempt to rule Europe through the Bonaparte clan and the family feuding that marked his reign. That story of personal acrimony is sometimes amusing, more often simply ugly. The medals tell only the beginning of the more poignant history of Napoleon's son who began life as the French 'King of Rome' and ended it as the Austrian Duke of Reichstadt.

The medals can tell us most about the women of Napoleon's family, how they were perceived by their contemporaries and to some extent how they saw themselves. Napoleon married Josephine Beauharnais in 1796, attracted by her beauty and charm, a few days before he left to take command of the French Army for the First Italian Campaign. Her beauty is not apparent on the coronation medal. Both the attributes are visible in a lovely large lead-gilt *cliché* by Andrieu, which he presented to her personally in 1807.[1] Beyond this she may be praised for her love of plants, exhibited at Malmaison, but not for her extravagant taste in clothes, which led to frequent quarrels with her husband. Her history is filled with stories of harassment by the Bonaparte women, who hated her. When they finally achieved their goal – Josephine's removal through divorce – their hatred was transferred to their new rival, Marie Louise.

Some time in the post-Josephine era, possibly in 1808, Denon conceived the idea of a series of small medals honouring the women of the imperial family, struck on the occasion of their (fictional) visits to the Medal Mint. Four charming 22mm portraits were produced with the ladies' titles in Greek letters and their hair arranged *a la grecque*. Later, a medal for Marie Louise was added (Br. 1303), the reverse with an inscription honouring her visit and with a finely detailed representation of a minting press. There are two reverse types for each of the other imperial women, one with a simple declaration that they visited the Mint and another with a design representing position, interest or accomplishments.

The story of Josephine's daughter Hortense, Queen of Holland (Br. 767) is a sad one. The fault in her case lies with the behaviour of her husband and Napoleon's brother, Louis, whom she did not wish to marry, who mistreated her and failed in his role as king. Her life might have been happy had she been allowed to pursue

NAPOLEON'S MEDALS: *Victory to the Arts*

THE EMPRESS JOSEPHINE (1805). By Andrieu and presented to her personally by the engraver. Heartily disliked by Napoleon's sisters but protected by her husband until he divorced her in 1809 when convinced she could not bear him a male heir. She died in 1814, shortly after his first abdication. (Andrieu; Br. 476), lead gilt *cliché*; 68mm.

unhindered the gifts celebrated on the reverse of her miniature medal, musical and painting paraphernalia arranged around an easel on which is hung a garland of roses. Below the easel is a book entitled *Romances* – ironic perhaps. Hortense did write her *Memoirs*[2] – a story without the happy ending one usually associates with romance.

Pauline was the prettiest of the sisters. Incapable of ruling anything, including herself and her passions, and interested only in pleasure, she pestered her brother until he made her Duchess of Guastala, an insignificant principality which she soon gave up in disgust. Her real accomplishment was to become an international beauty. For this achievement there is enduring evidence in Canova's celebrated half-nude statue of her as 'Venus Victorious', holding the golden apple awarded to her by Paris. She would naturally not consider Canova's original suggestion that she be carved as the chaste goddess Diana. It is reported that when asked by a friend if she did not feel uncomfortable posing in such attire, she replied, 'Not at all, there was a fire in the room.'

MARIE LOUISE OF AUSTRIA. Daughter of the Austrian Emperor. On Napoleon's abdication she ruled as Duchess of Parma, dying in 1847. (Andrieu; Br. 1303), 22mm.

HORTENSE. Daughter of Josephine. Greek inscription and coiffure in the Greek style. Unhappy wife of Louis, King of Holland, brother of Napoleon. On the reverse musical instruments and painting materials reflect her talents and a book, *ROMANCES*, references her literary interests. Her son, Louis, became Napoleon III. (Andrieu and Brenet; Br. 767), 22mm.

163

NAPOLEON'S MEDALS: *'Victory to the Arts'*

Pauline was the most outspoken in the irrational Bonaparte hatred of Josephine – she could never forgive her brother for making her carry Josephine's train at the coronation and is said to have yanked on it, almost making her fall. Yet there is a kind of redemption in the end of Pauline's story. While Caroline and Elisa betrayed Napoleon in order to save themselves in 1814, Pauline proved most loyal, selling her own jewels and going with him to Elba. The sensuous representation of the Three Graces on the reverse of her medal make quite clear the focus of her life, as does the legend, 'Beautiful One, Be Our Queen'.

The medal for Caroline, Queen of Naples, shows the man-headed bull being crowned by a Victory, the symbol of ancient Neapolis. The career of Caroline as Queen of Naples, with her husband the dashing Joachim Murat, is symptomatic of the failure of Napoleon's attempt to rule Europe through his family. In the end, Caroline and Murat turned against the Emperor in a vain attempt to save themselves.

PAULINE. Prettiest of the three Bonaparte sisters, who made a career as an international beauty, scandalising many with her immodest behaviour. The Three Graces, undraped, on the reverse are an appropriate comment on her lifestyle. 'Beautiful one be our Queen!' reads the Greek inscription (Andrieu; Br. 770), 22mm.

164

CAROLINE, Queen of Naples. Married to Joachim Murat, Napoleon's cavalry commander. One can imagine what kind of man Murat was from his reported last words, as he faced a firing squad in Calabria, having failed to regain the kingdom of Naples and Sicily: 'Save my face – aim for the chest – fire!' On the reverse is Victory crowning a man-headed bull, as on the coin of Naples. (Brenet; Br. 772), 22mm.

NAPOLEON'S MEDALS: *'Victory to the Arts'*

ELISA (Grand Duchess of Tuscany). Eldest and ablest of Napoleon's sisters, she brought order to her principality in northern Italy. She reopened the marble quarries at Carrara, doubled silk production and supported art, science, and industry. (Brenet; Br. 776), 22mm.

Elisa, the oldest of Napoleon's sisters, was the only one of his sisters to rule effectively. Given the principalities of Piombino, Luca, and Tuscany, she made considerable improvements in her kingdom, including the re-opening of the famous marble quarries at Cararra. The reverse of a medal celebrating the opening of the road from Pisa to Luca (Br. 774) reveals another of her accomplishments. The *denarius* of Trajan has Vibilia, Goddess of the Ways, reclining with her wheel. On Elisa's medal Vibilia reclines with a wheel, her back to a milestone. Another of Napoleon's medals, celebrating the opening of a coastal road from Nice to Rome (Br. 690), copies the Vibilia coin.

In March 1809, Napoleon created two battalions of Italian *Vélites* from annexed regions of the country; one, the *Vélites de Florence*, was for Elisa. The honour represented by the incorporation of the new battalion into the Imperial Guard was intended to mollify any local resentment of the annexation of Tuscany following the deposition of the previous ruler, Queen Maria Luisa of Etruria.[3]

Said to be most like Napoleon in personality, Elisa also resembled him physically. Her lovely portrait medal in this series, therefore, is surely flattering. A more accurate and more honest estimate of Elisa's features may be found in Mark Jones, No. 265, where she may be seen to resemble her brother.[4]

Captain Laskey has an interesting commentary on the medal of Elisa that shows how eager the English were to acquire French medals. It was reported that the medal for the Princess Elisa was 'deficient in every collection'. Two English gentlemen called on Andrieu, expressing an interest in the Elisa medal. Andrieu produced it, offering it for sale, 'and it was eventually purchased by them, and from them, at a very great price, by the publisher.'[5]

Notes

1 *Le Moniteur*, 29 April 1807. Something of the psychology of medal making is here revealed. Andrieu got free advertising and a notice that this medal, at a price of 10 francs together with those of the Battle of Marengo and the crossing of the St Bernard, were for sale.

2 *Mémoires de la reine Hortense.* (3 vols.) Paris, 1927. Cf. Constance Wright, *Daughter to Napoleon*. New York, 1961.

3 Andrew Uffindell, *Napoleon's Immortals*, 2007, p.66.

4 Mark Jones, *The Art of the Medal*, 1979, p.103.

5 Captain J.C. Laskey, *A Description of the Series of Medals Struck at the National Medal Mint by Order of Napoleon Bonaparte*, London, 1818, p.236.

XVI

The Royal Marriage

NAPOLEON AND MARIE LOUISE OF AUSTRIA (1810). (Andrieu; Br. 1100), 32mm.

The royal wedding of Napoleon and the Archduchess Marie Louise of Austria was the great event of the season. There was a call from the Emperor to Denon for medals in various sizes and metal equal to that of the coronation, 1,000 in gold, 4,000 in silver, and a great number of the smaller sizes.

The marriage was celebrated in stages. First a proxy wedding in Vienna on 11 of March and then the long journey to France. Marie Louise arrived in Strasbourg on 22 March 1810. The marriage itself took place on 1 April.

MARRIAGE IN VIENNA
Napoleon by proxy, (11 March 1810). Two torches united by a ribbon and *FELICIBUS NUPTIIS*. The reverse has *VOTA PUBLICA* in a wreath. (Br. 943), 28mm.

NAPOLEON'S MEDALS: *Victory to the Arts*

ARRIVAL AT STRASBOURG. The Empress arrived at Strasbourg on 22 March, on her journey to Paris. View of Strasbourg Cathedral. (Courtot; Br. 949), 32mm.

Denon's reply to Daru, Napoleon's Grand Marshal of the Palace, describes the medal for the wedding already in the process of execution. On the obverse are the conjoined heads of the Emperor and the Empress and on the reverse 'the Emperor in heroic costume conducting the Empress to the altar of Hymen'. The legend is '*PAX ET CONNUBIUM*'.[1] Denon's note describes accurately the wedding medal issued, except that the Latin phrase does not appear. Napoleon preferred French for all his public productions.

It is strange that the features on the 41mm medal by Joannin seem distorted. The 32mm piece, however, the reverse by Andrieu, is much more in keeping with the tradition of excellence in medal manufacture.

A letter to Daru of 8 March 1810 gives the total number of wedding medals finally struck – 85,000 in gold, silver, and bronze.[2] These were distributed to princes, ambassadors, persons of the Emperor's household, officials of the provinces and workers in the Mint. The tiny 15mm pieces were thrown to the crowds in public places.

MARRIAGE OF NAPOLEON AND MARIE LOUISE (1 April 1810). The couple in Roman dress before a lighted altar in an example of poor workmanship. (Jouannin; Br. 952)

MARRIAGE OF NAPOLEON AND MARIE LOUISE. Much better workmanship on this smaller medal. (Brenet; Br. 954), 32mm.

MARRIAGE OF NAPOLEON AND MARIE LOUISE. Small silver medal. According to Denon, 70,000 were struck to be thrown to the crowds. (Galle; Br. 956), 15mm.

NAPOLEON AND MARIE LOUISE (1510). Napoleon as King of Italy wears the Iron Crown, Marie Louise wears a diadem. (Manfredini; Br. 961)

THE ROYAL MARRIAGE

Manfredini in Milan issued a medal celebrating Napoleon's rule in Italy. He appears with Marie Louise, wearing the iron crown. On the reverse is Hymen with a torch chasing away Mars. What these medals, with their formal message, cannot reveal is the human factor, the real state of their marriage. Marie Louise's letters, discovered in the twentieth century, tell us that the marriage was in fact a happy one.

HYMEN CHASING MARS (1510). Hymen armed with a torch chases away Mars. (Manfredini; Br. 961)

Notes

1   De Fayolle, *Andrieu*, p.40.
2   De Fayolle, *Andrieu*, p.44.

XVII

The King of Rome

Marie Louise was most valuable to Napoleon as the mother of his son and heir. On a medal by Julien Marie Jouannin she is a Roman matron holding her son. Yet she was much more, a devoted and loyal wife through the dark days of 1814 and beyond – for a time. Her letters confirm her loyalty to Napoleon through his first exile and her desire to go to him on Elba.[1]

The sad end of the story is how Metternich, guardian of Austrian foreign policy, found a way to weaken that resolve through the introduction as her guardian of the dashing Colonel Niepperg, so that she finally not only abandoned her husband but declared that she had never loved him and is said to have rejoiced at the news of Waterloo. She was apparently popular as Duchess of Parma, but her letters reveal also a certain neglect of her son, who was compelled to remain in Vienna.

Soon after the birth of the King of Rome on 20 March 1811, Napoleon wrote to Josephine.

> My dear, I have received your letter, and thank you for it. My son is big and healthy. I hope he will come to some good. He has my chest, my mouth and my eyes. I hope he will fulfil his destiny.[2]

On the obverse of the medal with Marie Louise holding the child is a bust of the infant with his titles, *NAPOLEON FRANCOIS JOSEPH CHARLES ROI DE ROME.* Another view of the boy (Br. 1108) features him as the infant Hercules, strangling snakes in his cradle, copying many ancient representations on coins and in painting. A tiny 16mm medal (Br. 1094) shows the King of Rome suckled by the Roman wolf. There is, of course, only one infant replacing the twins Romulus and Remus.

A splendid 68mm medal designed by Lafitte and engraved by Andrieu depicts the baptism of the King of Rome on 9 June 1811. Napoleon, in imperial costume, standing between throne and baptismal font, raises the child high in the air. The reverse of the medal contains an inscription, *A L'EMPEREUR LES BONNES VILLES DE L'EMPIRE,* the symbols for the cities arranged in two rings around the inscription. At the audience after the parade, 'the good cities of the Empire' who had sent representatives to the ceremony, presented the medal to the Emperor.

MARIE LOUISE AS A ROMAN MATRON, holding the king of Rome, born 20 March 1811. Named Napoleon Francis Joseph Charles. (Jouannin; Br. 1099)

THE KING OF ROME (Galle, Tiolier; Br. 1094), 16mm.

NAPOLEON'S MEDALS: *Victory to the Arts*

THE KING OF ROME AND THE ROMAN WOLF. The wolf, naturally, suckles only one royal child. (Galle, Tiolier; Br. 1094), 16mm.

There are several reports of the ceremony and its aftermath.

The acclamation of the congregation echoed through the cathedral and grew louder when Napoleon, after kissing his son three times, was suddenly overcome by emotion, and drunk with joy and pride, his heart beating wildly, raised the little King high above him, as if to show the people the future sovereign of the Western Empire.[3]

Immediately after the baptism[4] the governess

> placed the king in the hands of the Empress. M. Duverdier, Chief Herald of Arms advanced to the centre of the choir and cried three times 'Long live the King of Rome!' These cries repeated by all the spectators, were prolonged for a very long time, during which the Empress, standing, held her child in her arms.

The Emperor was very much touched by that response.

We overtake the history of Napoleon, the disastrous Russian expedition and the campaigns in Germany of 1813, which saw the retreat to France, in order

THE KING OF ROME

to follow the fortunes of the King of Rome. We begin in January 1814 with Napoleon facing Allied armies closing in on France from the East.

We see him on a medal (Br 1333) leaving from St Cloud to join the Army on 25 January. The scene is pictured as a poignant farewell. Napoleon dressed as a Greek warrior entrusts his son to Marie Louise and the city of Paris before leaving to face the enemy. The last farewell was actually his final view of the sleeping child before the predawn departure. The boy's affection for his father is expressed in the outstretched arm.

Marie Louise's letters to Napoleon at the front in this last campaign are full of the young Napoleon's expressions of love for his absent father, as they are of her own love for her husband.

BAPTISM OF THE KING OF ROME (9 June 1811). Napoleon before a throne lifts the infant above the baptismal font. The reverse has 49 mural crowns representing the cities that had sent representatives to the ceremony. Signed by the artist Lafitte, and the engraver Andrieu. (Br. 1125), 68mm.

NAPOLEON'S MEDALS: *'Victory to the Arts'*

NAPOLEON LEAVES FROM ST CLOUD (January 1814). Napoleon dressed as a Greek warrior gives his son to Paris and to Marie Louise. The child seems reluctant to leave his father. (Brenet; Br. 1333)

Your son is as good as ever and has asked me to tell you that he had eaten all his spinach. That may not appear very interesting to you, but it is great news for him as it means that he has conquered an aversion.

When he awoke on 4 February 1814, Marie Louise wrote to Napoleon that the boy declared, 'I have had a dream. I went to see Papa at Chalons and I asked dear Papa to come back quickly and he came back with me.'

'You see how much he thinks about you, even when he is asleep,' she continued. 'This love he bears you makes him dearer than ever to me.'[5] The Empress and her little King became hopeful at the news of Napoleon's victories over the invading Allied armies, the last of which came on the child's third birthday, 20 March 1814. A letter that she wrote to her husband on that occasion seems prophetic of her later behaviour. The boy had so pestered his mother to tell him where his birthday presents were that she had finally given in. 'You can see that I am not very strong-willed. And so I have decided to spoil him as much as I can for a few more years.'[6]

The Allied armies now closed in; Marie Louise and the King of Rome fled Paris, which fell to the enemy. While Napoleon was able to maintain a defensive position at Fontainebleau, there was talk of a regency of Marie Louise with her son. But when this collapsed, he was obliged to abdicate (on 11 April) with only minor concessions. Napoleon was to receive the island of Elba as his kingdom and Marie Louise and her son would receive the principality of Parma.

The young Napoleon and his mother were taken to Vienna by the Austrians. Marie Louise at first hoped and planned, as her letters reveal, to join her husband on Elba, continuing to prove her love and loyalty to him. Too soon, however, she yielded to the charms of General Niepperig. When, on her son's fourth birthday, Napoleon's letter arrived announcing his approach to Paris and inviting her to come to the capital with her son, she was no longer interested in going – even had she been able to.

The environment in which her young son now lived is reflected in his outburst at Schoenbrunn on 21 July, where in response to talk among his attendants about Waterloo and its aftermath he said, 'My dear Papa is a wicked man. So will they kill him?'[7] On 2 September, in response to an inquiry about the boy's education, Marie Louise wrote:

> You ask me what I mean when I say that I intend to have him brought up according to the principles of my native land: I mean that I want to make a German prince out of him, as good and honest as the rest; and when he grows up I want him to serve his new country.[8]

During the early phases of the return from Elba, Napoleon seems to have had some hope of restoring his son to the line of succession. His proclamation of 'the Field of May' made from Lyon, suggests that. But by 1 June, when 'the Field of May' was finally held, it had become simply, or rather elaborately, a declaration of support for the constitution.

The Emperor, meanwhile, had been informed by his faithful secretary, Meneval, arriving from Vienna in the middle of May, of the true situation there. Nevertheless, when after Waterloo he abdicated a second time (22 June 1815), he did so in favour of his son: 'My political life is over and I proclaim my son Napoleon II Emperor of the French.'[9]

Napoleon can hardly have had much hope his wish would be fulfilled, much less the Deputies, who reluctantly agreed. The medal by Henrionnet with the effigy of the four-year-old Napoleon was struck proclaiming the myth that 'Napoleon F.J.C. King of Rome' had become on 23 June 1815, 'Emperor of the French'. The medallic image was undoubtedly imaginary since the artist could not have seen the boy for over a year.[10] Equally fictitious was the scene on Brenet's medal in which 'Napoleon gives his son to France.'

The subsequent history of Napoleon's son lies beyond the scope of this narrative. He was, as Marie Louise had promised, brought up as a German prince. He was now called 'Francis' and received the meaningless title of 'Duke of Reichstadt' to

'PROCLAIMED EMPEROR OF THE FRENCH', 23 June 1815. A desperate attempt to continue the dynasty that could not succeed. (Henrionnet; Br. 1667), 26mm.

THE KING OF ROME (1815) at four years of age. (Henrionnet; Br. 1667), 26mm.

THE KING OF ROME

replace 'Prince of Parma', when it was decided that he was not to be allowed to succeed his mother who had become Duchess of Parma, or even to accompany her to her new home. Marie Louise left for the pleasures of Parma and the company of Neipperg, whom she eventually married, neglecting the boy in Vienna. In Vienna, the young Francis Charles grew up as an Austrian prince, his ambition to become an officer in the Austrian Army.

However, the changing political situation in Europe, the new independence of several European countries, Belgium, Greece, and Poland, and the turmoil surrounding the July Revolution of 1830 in France, with the appearance of a Bonapartist faction, suddenly created new opportunities for the charming young man with the famous name.

The Austrian court was not entirely averse to the idea that Napoleon's son should be king of France, since his loyalty to Austria was assumed – correctly, for all that we can tell. But though Bonapartists in France and revolutionaries in Italy called for Napoleon II to be their king, and the daughter of Napoleon's sister, Elisa – whose name was 'Napoleone' – proposed a mysterious intrigue in his name, the real opportunity never presented itself. His fate was finally sealed by the tuberculosis that finally brought his life to an end on 22 July 1832 at the age of 21.

In May 1826, the English Baronet, Sir Horace David Cholwell St Paul, paid a visit to Francis I Emperor of Austria, who received him graciously for the sake of his father, Horace St Paul, who had fought for him in the Seven Years War. For this service the elder St Paul had been given the title of Count of the Holy Roman Empire. On his way to Vienna, the Baronet stopped at Parma, where he dined with Marie Louise, now Duchess of Parma, and later in Vienna met the former Napoleon II, by then the Duke of Reichstadt. He noted in his diary that 'the eyes of the young Napoleon are light blue like his mother's whose countenance he more resembles than his father's.'[11] But perhaps the young Napoleon resembled his father more than his mother in character and ability – a question for which circumstances and the politics of the time precluded a definitive proof.

NAPOLEON GIVES HIS SON TO FRANCE (1815). The second abdication. The boy, now four years old, looks back at his father in apprehension. In fact the boy and his mother had been in Austria for a year. (Brenet; Br. 1664)

181

Notes

1. Most of this personal narrative concerning Marie Louise and her son is from André Castelot, *King of Rome, A Biography of Napoleon's Tragic Son*, translated by Robert Baldick. New York: Harper & Brothers, 1960. Castelot's major source is the newly discovered letters.
2. Castelot, *King of Rome*, p.49.
3. Castelot, *King of Rome*, p.55.
4. De Foyelle, *Andrieu*, p.52.
5. All from Castelot, *King of Rome*, pp.88–89.
6. From Castelot.
7. Castelot, p.176.
8. Castelot, p.179.
9. Castelot, p.173.
10. Castelot, p.66, suggests that the image may have been adapted from a painting, perhaps by Gerard.
11. George G. Butler, ed., *Colonel St Paul of Ewart, Soldier and Diplomat*. The St Catherine Press and James Nisbet & Co., 2 vols., 1911. Vol. I, p.clxxix.

XVIII

Star of Destiny

When Napoleon Bonaparte was proclaimed Consul for Life on 15 August 1802, the night of celebration that followed was illuminated by fireworks and Napoleon's star – 'thirty feet in height, gleaming above the towers of Notre Dame'.[1] Throughout his life, Bonaparte trusted his 'star' – his good fortune, his destiny.

Two images of ships, both by Brenet, frame Napoleon's confidence in his fortune. A medal struck in 'the year 4 of Bonaparte' (Br. 275) pictures Fortune in a bark, guided by Napoleon's star, in full sail on a calm sea. The dedication is *A LA FORTUNE CONSERVATRICE*. Some suggest confidence in a successful invasion of England; the date of 1804 shows the timing is right. Scargill's commentary, followed by Griffiths, discerns gratitude for protection from the plot

A LA FORTUNE CONSERVATRICE (1804). Fortune, 'the Protector' sets sail with a fair wind, destination not specified. Napoleon's lucky star is in the field, which protected him for a decade. Napoleon's portrait resembling Augustus – another fortunate ruler – is on the other side. (Brenet; Br. 275), 34mm.

183

NAPOLEON'S MEDALS: *Victory to the Arts*

FORTUNE ADVERSE (March 1814). On a ship with a broken steering oar and a broken wheel in the field. Capitulation of Paris in March of 1814. Fortune now betrays her favourite. (Brenet; Br. 1365)

of 3 Nivose. Another ship from the very end of Napoleon's reign, with Fortune, her back turned (Br. 1365), is drifting aimlessly with a broken oar, a broken wheel in the field, and captioned FORTUNE ADVERSE.

Napoleon's faith in his star was not blind. He felt that his own actions were of equal importance in confronting the lot fortune had dealt him. 'For all the faith I have in French valour, I have good faith in my lucky star, or perhaps in myself, and as a result, I never count positively on victory unless I am in command.'[2] Nevertheless, Napoleon was conscious that at critical points in his career his good fortune had intervened conspicuously, perhaps miraculously, to protect

STAR OF DESTINY

him or to further his cause. Perhaps Josephine also believed – at her wedding she wore around her neck a necklace of chains of her hair with a medallion on which was engraved 'To Destiny'.[3] Napoleon's medallists understood this faith in his lucky star.

Bonaparte's dangerous return to France from Egypt with a small flotilla, arriving on 9 October 1799 and eluding the British navy, is commemorated on a medallion that celebrates his good fortune (H. 921). Several small ships are shown approaching the harbor at Frejus, on the south coast near Cannes; Bonaparte's star is in the heavens. On the reverse is the Roman god, *BONUS EVENTUS*.

This medal, not struck until 1806, has another curious and less noble connection with destiny. We know from an archival note of 7 September 1807 by First Chamberlain, Remusat[4] that he had received 200 *Bonus Eventus* medals ordered by His Majesty for use at his gaming tables! This is confirmed by a receipt in the French archives.

The Cisalpine Republic, in northern Italy, was revived by the Convention of Alessandria (16 June 1800), which ended the victorious Second Italian Campaign. On a medallion commemorating the event (Br. 42) but remembering the Battle of

ARRIVAL AT FREJUS
Bonaparte's 'good luck'. Having escaped from Egypt and the British fleet with four small ships, the squadron approaches the harbour on 9 October 1799. Bonaparte's star is in the heavens. (Galle; H. 921), 33mm.

NAPOLEON'S MEDALS: *'Victory to the Arts'*

THE ROMAN GOD, BONUS EVENTUS. God of good luck holding a *patera* and an ear of corn. From an ancient statue. Actually struck years later. Napoleon once ordered a large number in silver to use as gaming pieces. (Galle; H. 921), 33mm.

Marengo that made it possible, Hercules raises a maiden representing the Cisalpine Republic. In the background is the sun with Napoleon's star at its centre. The Cisalpine Republic came to an end in 1802 when Bonaparte incorporated it into the Italian Republic (Br. 189).

On 24 December 1800, a royalist 'infernal machine', a powder keg planted in a wagon placed to block Napoleon's route to the opera, only missed Bonaparte because the assassin's timing was off. Napoleon's version of the event, related on St Helena, was that his drunken coachman whipped up the horses and crowded past the obstruction. Napoleon, napping, was awakened by the pitching of the carriage, thinking at first that he was back in Italy, 'at a time when he had ordered his coachman to ford a flooded river at night and the going had been rough.' He was far enough beyond the cart when it exploded so that only his rear guard was shaken up.

Manfredini's medal for the event, from Appiani's drawing, shows Destiny and the three Fates. Clotho holds the distaff, Lachesis forms the thread and Atropos holds the spindle on which she places the thread. Destiny holds the scissors, but refuses to cut the thread. The obverse has a bust of Bonaparte with his lucky star in the field.

A more personal medal was struck for the occasion (Br. 76). It expressed *THE LOVE OF THE FRENCH PEOPLE FOR THE FIRST CONSUL*. The reverse has an inscription with noble words attributed to Bonaparte. As 'a crowd of citizens rushed to him' he said, *FRIENDS, IT IS NOT I TO WHOM YOU SHOULD COME; GO AND HELP THOSE UNFORTUNATES WHOM THE INFERNAL MACHINE WAS ABLE TO HIT.*

ASSASSINATION ATTEMPT OF DECEMBER 1800

Obverse, head of Bonaparte, his lucky star in the field. Reverse, Destiny and the Three Fates. Destiny holds the shears but will not cut the cord held by the Fates. On 24 December 1800 Royalist assassins exploded a cask of gunpowder near his carriage as he was being driven to the Opera. Fortunately, their timing was off and Bonaparte escaped injury. (Napoleon later said the driver was drunk and drove too fast.) (Appiani; Manfredini; Br. 77), 59mm.

That Napoleon accepted the ship image as a representation for his life and career is supported by a conversation reported by Las Casas (11 November 1816).

> I may have had many projects but I never was free to carry out any of them. It did me little good to be holding the helm; no matter how strong my hands the sudden and numerous waves were stronger still, and I was wise enough to yield to them rather than resist them obstinately and make the ship founder.

The obverse of Manfredini's beautiful *VINDOBONA CAPTA* medal (Br. 444) pictures Napoleon in an outlandish helmet, perhaps Athena's. On the visor is his star.

Napoleon's good fortune protected him in battle until the end of his military career, though he often exposed himself to enemy fire. Sometimes Fortuna awarded him a victory when circumstances, or even his own lapse of judgment, brought him face to face with defeat. At the Battle of Essling in the campaign of 1809 Napoleon's over-audacious crossing of the Danube brought near disaster, when the angry river (Br. 859) swept away a pontoon bridge. Bonaparte's fortune saved him from his own folly when the able Archduke Charles unaccountably failed to follow up his victory.

Napoleon's Russian campaign began well enough with the taking of Wilna in present-day Lithuania and through the Battle of Borodino, when Hercules fought for the French (Br. 1162). But Napoleon's decision to remain too long in Moscow and wait for a willingness to negotiate from the Emperor Alexander doomed him to the ravages of the Russian winter of 1812. The medallist could blame the disastrous defeat on the unusually severe winter, Boreas with his bag of winds blowing cold and death on the retreating army, the field littered with broken wagons and dead horses.

Napoleon knew better; it was his own folly in staying too long in Moscow hoping for Russian capitulation. Ségur reports a conversation with the Emperor on 23 October 1812.

> And he could not even blame his star. Had not the sun of France followed him into Russia? ... It was not his luck that had failed him. Was it he who had failed his luck?[5]

The sequel of the Russian debacle of the winter of 1812 was a rapid decline in Napoleon's fortunes through the spring of 1813, punctuated by an occasional victory, duly commemorated by his engravers. On 2 May 1813 he defeated the Russians and the Prussians at Lützen. A medal shows a Russian Cossack and a Prussian cavalryman fleeing before French infantry. The victory of Wurtchen (or Bautzen) on 20/21 May is celebrated by a medal with a stack of muskets on a mound of enemy spoil, and the significant inscription, *INFANTRIE FRANCAISE. BATAILLE DE WURTCHEN*. The victory is attributed to the

TAKING OF WILNA

Napoleon's last success before the Russian disaster. Two Polish chiefs in national costume take an oath with Napoleon (28 June 1812). (Andrieu; Br. 1156)

RETREAT FROM RUSSIA. Boreas with his bag of winds blows death and destruction on a Russian soldier. November 1812. For the ful medal see p.57. (Galle; Br. 1168)

NAPOLEON'S MEDALS: *'Victory to the Arts'*

French infantry; Napoleon had been unable to make good the terrible loss of horses in the Russian retreat.

From the battlefield of Wurtchen, on 22 May, Napoleon issued a decree for the erection of a monument on Mount Cenis,[6] directed to the Institute of France, the Kingdom of Italy, the Academies of Rome, Amsterdam, Turin, and Florence. A supplement to the decree decided what should go on the mountain.

> On the face of the monument on the side of Paris, will be inscribed the names of all of our cantons of the departments on this side of the Alps. On the face that faces Milan, will be inscribed the names of all the cantons beyond the Alps and of our kingdom of Italy … as a witness to the memory of his people of France and of Italy and in order to transmit to the most remote posterity the memory of that celebrated epoch when in three months one million two hundred thousand men ran to arms to ensure the integrity of the territory of the Empire and of her allies.

BATTLE OF LÜTZEN (2 May 1813). A Cossack and a Prussian cavalryman flee before the French infantry. (Brenet; Br. 1229)

Whether Napoleon had any intention of erecting such a monument is doubtful, but the dutiful Denon produced a medal with the necessary inscription, 'one million two hundred thousand men', rushing to the defence of the Empire and a splendid mountain with an eagle at its summit. The monument would be as much of a reality as those one million men.

BATTLE OF WURTCHEN (20 May 1813). A stack of muskets on a mound of enemy spoil. After Lützen and Wurtchen was the moment of truth: would Napoleon's father-in-law, the Emperor Francis, abandon him? (Brenet: Br. 1232)

MONUMENT ON MOUNT CENIS. After the Battle of Wurtchen Napoleon ordered an eagle placed on top of Mount Cenis on an imperial throne, looking toward Paris on the one side and toward Milan on the other. On the medal an inscription told how in three months France and Italy had armed 'one million, two hundred thousand men for the defence of the empire'. The dutiful Denon had the medal struck, but of course the monument was never built. (Brenet; Br. 1233)

NAPOLEON'S MEDALS: *Victory to the Arts*

Napoleon's star did not come to his aid through the remainder of 1813 and the first months of 1814. The German and Russian medals are much more numerous than those of the French for the rest of 1813, since the Allies had the advantage. The Battle of Leipzig, 16–19 October, pictured on a German medal (Br. 1259) was decisive, forcing Napoleon to retreat. Another German medal pictures a vain attempt to stem the Allied advance at Hanau on 30 October (Br. 1273). On the obverse of the medal the three victorious sovereigns hold hands as a symbol of their unity.

The early months of 1814 saw Napoleon desperately trying to defend the French homeland. A medallion (Br. 1333) pictures Napoleon's departure from St Cloud on 26 January to join the Army. The Emperor, in Greek military costume, hands over his son and Marie Louise to the protection of the city of Paris. The child holds out an arm in a touching appeal to his father. Napoleon, in flashes of his old brilliance, won four battles in February in five days at Champaubert, Montmirail, Chateau-Thierry and Vauchamps against the invading armies, but he could not prevail against the overwhelming force of the Allies. Paris fell on 30 March.

Finally, as we have seen, Fortune finally turns her back on her favourite. The second ship medal by Brenet shows her adrift in a boat, driven aimlessly, the steering oar broken as is her wheel, with Napoleon's star in its centre. The legend reads FORTUNE ADVERSE MARS MDCCCXIV.

BATTLE OF LEIPZIG (19 October 1813). A Prussian eagle hovers over the city and the battlefield. It was the decisive Allied victory that forced Napoleon's withdrawal to France. (Stettner; Br. 1259), AE silvered, 33mm.

BATTLE OF HANAU

(30 October 1813). Prussian and Russian eagles watch over the end of Napoleon's European hegemony. A delaying action that could not stem the Allied advance. *Lieutenant* Frédéric-Jacques Rilliet de Constant described how at Hanau, 'The [Imperial] Guard cavalry came forward as if it was certain of victory and there was no need to hurry.' The victorious Allied sovereigns hold hands on the reverse. (Lauer; Br. 1273), AE silvered, 33mm.

NAPOLEON'S MEDALS: *Victory to the Arts*

NAPOLEON ABDICATES (11 April 1814). Napoleon at a writing desk signs the decree which a Fury, standing behind holding a torch, dictates. Alternatively it could depict the Emperor trying to restrain the Fury (Discord?) who wants to prevent the signing. (Brenet; Br. 1386)

On 11 April Napoleon abdicated. According to Brenet's engraving a Fury behind him dictates while he writes, or on another view, attempts to prevent him from signing. A crude English satirical medal marks Bonaparte's departure for Elba. Napoleon rides backwards on a donkey led by the devil. *INSEPARABLE FRIENDS* and *TO ELBA* read the inscriptions. On the reverse are the names of the victorious allied sovereigns who insist, *WE CONQUER TO SET FREE*.

The allied leaders enjoyed the sights of the capital. On 27 April Francis I visited the Museum of Fine Arts and the Gallery of Models. The Emperor was particularly taken by the ruins of Pola and Spoleto and asked for a catalogue. These were probably the models used for the images of the Temple of Augustus at Pola and the Palace of Diocletian at Spoleto on medals commemorating the ceding of Istria (Br. 512) and Dalmatia (Br. 513) to France as a result of Austerlitz.[7]

Fredrick William III, King of Prussia visited the Mint where the medals were made. He was presented with one with his image on one side and on the other a note of his visit. He was impressed with the likeness and commended the engraver, Gayrard.[8]

194

TO ELBA (1814). British satirical medal. Napoleon riding backwards on a donkey led by the Devil – *INSEPARABLE FRIENDS*. On the reverse the names of the victors. (T. Kettle; Br. 1415), 25mm.

FREDERICK WILIAM III, KING OF PRUSSIA, VISITS THE MINT (1814). *Le Moniteur* reported that he was pleased with the portrait medal presented to him by Denon. (Gayrard; Br. 1466)

HISTORY (OR VICTORY) WRITING ON A TABLET, sitting in the shade of an olive tree seated on a cube decorated with a serpent eating his tail. She writes *SEJOUR D'ALEX. I A PARIS.* (Andrieu, Br. 1464)

STAR OF DESTINY

The Emperor Alexander I of Russia visited the Museum of Natural History and on 28 May the *Monnaie des Médailles*. He was flattered to receive from the Director of the Mint a piece with Peter the Great on one side and his own portrait on the other.[9]

As previously mentioned, there was one other incident involving Alexander that indicates the breadth of his interests. He visited Ecouen and had lunch with Mme. Campan, the famous proprietor. He was impressed with her arrangements and told her that there were many parallels with a similar house that the Queen, his mother, had founded in St Petersburg.[10]

STAY OF ALEXANDER I IN PARIS (1814). The Emperor of Russia came to Paris at Napoleon's abdication in April 1814 and stayed to have his portrait done by Andrieu. He received a tour of the Mint. (Andrieu; Br. 1464)

NAPOLEON'S MEDALS: *Victory to the Arts*

LOUIS XVIII WELCOMED BY FRANCE (1814). France, a woman in ancient dress wearing the royal crown, welcomes an approaching ship with open arms. 'He bears the peace of the world.' (Brenet; Br. 1406)

There is one final chapter in the Allied triumph, the British re-occupation of Hanover. On a medal by Webb and Barre, the Duke of Cambridge who was forced to leave when the French took over the country in 1803 was restored to his position as Governor General. On the reverse Britannia, the British Lion at her feet, earnestly feeds two horses.

The king, Louis XVIII, arrived at Calais on 24 April. *IL PORTE LA PAIX DU MONDE*, his medal declares. He was welcomed by a huge throng of people symbolised by a maiden wearing a crown. A grand ceremony for the King's arrival in Paris was planned according to an elaborate programme.

THE DUKE OF CAMBRIDGE. Youngest brother of George III. Originally in charge of the defence of Hanover, he was forced to leave when the French took over the Electorate in 1803. When the country was recovered in 1814 he was restored to his position as Governor General. (Webb; Br. 1489)

THE BRITISH RE-ENTER HANOVER (1814). Britannia, the lion at her feet, 'giving succour to the Hanoverian horses', Mudie, p.126. (Barre; Br. 1489)

Notes

1. Bourienne, in F. Moussiker, p.250.
2. Christopher Herold, *The Mind of Napoleon*, New York, 1955. p.219. (Conversation, 1803).
3. Alan Schom, *Napoleon Bonaparte*. New York, 1937, p.35. According to F. Mossiker, 'Napoleon gave Josephine as a wedding present a gold wedding band ... slipped on the bride's finger – a ring engraved "To Destiny", which would be worn as a talisman on the finger of Josephine's grandson when he entered Paris as emperor in 1851.'
4. J.J. Guiffrey, 'La Monnaie des Médailles,' *Revue Numismatique*, 3rd series, vol. IV, p.98.
5. Recorded in Herold, *The Mind of Napoleon*, p.45.
6. *Le Moniteur*, 11 June 1813.
7. *Le Moniteur*, 28 April 1814.
8. *Le Moniteur*, 8 May 1814.
9. *Le Moniteur*, 26 May 1814.
10. *Journal anecdotique de Mme Campan. Par M. Maigne, Médecin des Hôpitaux de Nantes*. Paris, 1824, pp.46–50.

XIX

The Hundred Days

The crowned eagle flying from Elba to the French mainland carries in its beak the original Legion of Honour.[1] The reason is clear. Louis XVIII had reorganised the Legion into one that suited him (Br. 1482). Placing the portrait of Henry IV, the national hero, on the obverse, he changed the reverse into the symbol of the French monarchy, a crowned *fleur-de-lis*. In addition, Louis had discontinued the stipend that was an original part of the award. Furthermore, in place of the Old Guard, now disbanded, a new order of young notables was created.

A CROWNED EAGLE FLYING WITH THE ORIGINAL LEGION OF HONOUR IN ITS BEAK (1815). Louis XVIII had reorganised the original Legion of Honour. On the medal he had replaced Napoleon's portrait with that of Henry IV. On the reverse a crown above an identical double five-pointed star, but within the circle a *fleur-de-lis* has replaced the Napoleonic eagle. The eagle flies from Elba in the distance, and approaches the French shore holding the original Legion of Honour. (Br. 1482)

NAPOLEON'S MEDALS: *Victory to the Arts*

Napoleon knew that his appeal to the soldiers to take up again the 'Eagles ... of Ulm, Austerlitz, Jena, Eylau, Friedland, Tudela, Eckmuhl, Essling, Wagram, Smolensk, Moskow, Lützen, Wurschen, Montmirail,'[2] would be received with acclamation. He had only to overcome the resistance of the officers.

Fortunately for Napoleon, Louis XVIII had difficulty finding officers that had not been members of Napoleon's team. That Napoleon had judged correctly the triumphant effect of his eighteen-day march to Paris 'without a shot being fired' is proof enough. The Eagle with the Tricolour would, as he promised his soldiers, adorn the towers of Notre Dame.[3]

The medallion that pictures the monument, presumably built in the Gulf of Juan where Napoleon landed, is interesting because there is no evidence that a monument was ever built there. However, *Le Moniteur* of 21 May 1815 explains the intent behind the deed and the inscription *CVI* (106) on the medallion.[4]

THE LEGION OF HONOUR (1804). A double-rayed five-pointed star surrounded by branches of oak and laurel around a circle with the words *HONNEUR ET PATRIE*. Within the circle an eagle holds a thunderbolt in its talons. Around the edge the claim *AUSPICE NEAPOLEONE GALLIA RENOVATA*. The Legion of Honour was proposed in May 1802, but the first decorations were awarded on 15 July 1804. In 1814 Louis XVIII reorganised the Legion. Napoleon's eagle, returning to France in 1815, carries the original insignia of the Legion. (Jaley; Br. 310)

202

THE HUNDRED DAYS

The 106th regiment of the line in the garrison of Antibes, full of devotion to the Emperor, wanting to transmit to posterity the happy event which has brought him back to the soil of the fatherland, has resolved to erect, at their common expense, a monument on the place where, on the first of March 1815, Napoleon landed, on his return from the Island of Elba; on the place where, near the sea and the highway, under an olive tree, happy symbol of peace, he bivouacked the following night, with the 1140 soldiers who always accompanied him …

On the fourth of May the regiment, wanting to proceed to the inauguration of the same monument, took up arms, preceded by the drums and the band and followed by two cannon, marched at noon to the Gulf of Juan to the place intended for it. There they found the military, administrative, and judicial authorities, and a number of the inhabitants of the town and of the surrounding communes. After many speeches and the *Domine salvum fac Imperatorem*, chanted by the curé of Valeuris, the colonel, acting in the name of the regiment, laid the first stone of the monument, accompanied by many discharges of artillery and muskets, to the sound of war-like music, and cries of *vive l'Empereur*, repeated a thousand times by all the military, by the magistrates and by the citizens who were present.

No remains are to be found. As in the case of the monuments to heroes ordered for the celebration of 1800, 'the first stone' was seen as sufficient promise of the monument to come. However, this brief account of one regiment's devotion to the Emperor expresses very well how it was that Napoleon was able to march to Paris and attach to himself the loyalty of a nation.

THE GULF OF JUAN MONUMENT. Around the edge, *A NAPOLEON LE CVI. REG.* The 106th Regiment of Antibes, determined to mark the place where Napoleon landed on his return from Elba, sponsored an elaborate ceremony in which the first stone for the monument was laid. (Br. 1590), 28mm.

NAPOLEON'S MEDALS: *'Victory to the Arts'*

RETURN OF NAPOLEON (March 1815). Napoleon in military dress welcomed by a French Grenadier and a peasant – the army and the people. (Andrieu; Br. 1591)

A medal commemorates the reception he received from both the soldiery and the people. The reverse of the flight from Elba medal has Napoleon in military dress being welcomed by a Grenadier and a peasant, representing the people. Napoleon had chosen his route well, avoiding regions in the hostile south where he had been threatened on his journey into exile. He avoided large towns, proceeding north by way of Grasse and Lafferty. The real test would be Grenoble, where there was a substantial garrison, but Napoleon had been in correspondence with Colonel La Bedoyere who arrived with his regiment in time to escort him into the city. With a substantially augmented force he now proceeded to Lyons, which he reached on 10 March and entered unopposed. As we have seen, Napoleon had presciently cultivated a special relationship with Lyons, taking time after the victory at Marengo in June 1800 to visit the city and participate in the reconstruction of the city centre. The city did not disappoint him, refusing to respond to the Count d'Artois' call for *Vive le Roi*, they reserved their shouts of *Vive l'Empereur* for Napoleon's appearance the next day in the Place Bellecour, the very place where he had laid the first stone fifteen years earlier.

THE HUNDRED DAYS

From Lyons Napoleon issued on 13 March a decree dissolving the current legislature and including his proposal for an *Assemblée Extraordinaire du Champ de Mai*, to take up measures to correct and modify the constitution, and at the same time to attend the coronation of the 'Empress, our dear and beloved spouse and that of our dear and beloved son'.

The tiny medal (13mm) which appeared in celebration of the Field of May is not so grand as either the pretension of the decree or as a description of the splendid ceremonies that eventually took place on the field of May on 1 June. The obverse of the medal has a bust of Napoleon with the simple description, 'Emperor', an indication, as he pretended, of his limited intentions – he had given up a claim to be King of Italy and the new constitution seemed to promise a limited monarchy.

But the question of actual intent was far from settled; Napoleon immediately embarked on a programme of conscription and organisation that produced in a surprisingly short time an army of 284,000. It was a portion of that army that he led into Belgium in pursuit of Wellington.

THE FIELD OF MAY
Announced from Lyons, the grand assembly in May was an occasion to amend the French constitution and for the coronation of the Empress and the King of Rome. It finally took place, but as a grand celebration of the new constitution. (Br. 1632), 13mm.

205

NAPOLEON'S MEDALS: *Victory to the Arts*

WATERLOO MEDAL
Ordered by the Prince Regent in 1819, engraved by Benedetto Pistrucci over a period of 30 years but never struck. A half-size copy was produced by Pinches in 1966. The obverse features the heads of the four victorious monarchs flanked by Hercules and Justice. Above the sun (or Apollo) drives a chariot preceded by the Dioscuri. Below, Night rides in a *biga*, AR 64mm.

The news of Napoleon's landing at the Gulf of Juan reached Paris on 5 March, but the response of the King was never swift enough to match the speed of Napoleon's movement or to cope with the number of desertions from his own forces. *Le Moniteur* was filled with useless declarations of loyalty to the crown. Finally, on the 21st *Le Moniteur* declared 'The King and the Princes have left in the night.' That issue of *Le Moniteur* contained various proclamations, some ostensibly from the Gulf of Juan and others from Lyons dissolving the government of the King and establishing a new imperial government.

In spite of Napoleon's promise of peace he certainly knew that war was inevitable, indeed that parts of his own country were in rebellion against him. Badly in need of money, he mothballed almost the entire fleet so as not to have that expense. By sometimes ruthless methods he managed to get enough money for his purposes. The men he needed for his army were harder to obtain, but by rounding up old soldiers and by a new subscription list of the class of 1815 he managed to assemble the 284,000 previously mentioned. Of these, 105,000 were needed to put down internal uprisings and a good part of the remainder were required to defend the frontiers.

THE HUNDRED DAYS

The army was ready by 1 June. It is significant that most of his letters in April and May were to his immediate subordinates responsible for organising the war effort, to Carnot, Minister of the Interior and particularly to Davout, Minister of War. But Napoleon needed popular support. The 'Additional Act, to the Constitutions of the Empire' did not meet with universal consent, but was approved anyway on the 'Field of May', the grand ceremony held on 1 June. It was introduced by the roar of cannon, begun the night before at the Tuileries and echoed throughout the city.

If the small 13mm medal was inadequate to celebrate so grand an event as the *Champ de Mai* turned out to be, there were other medals commemorating both it and the constitution (e.g. Br. 1628). The eagle with spread wings is appropriate for a ceremony which featured the distribution of the eagles to the troops. No one noticed, or if they did so did not comment, on the absence of 'my beloved spouse' or 'my beloved son', who were to be honoured at the ceremony as promised in the declaration from Lyons. As so often in the past, the fate of the constitution and of the nation depended on the outcome of the immediate campaign.

REVERSE OF THE PISTURCCI MEDAL
Wellington and Blucher on horseback guided by Victory. Jupiter in a *quadriga* throws a thunderbolt at a circle of giants.

The story of the subsequent events, the Battles of Ligny and Quatre Bras, and of Waterloo, have been told often, and retold and illustrated on medals. One medal intended to speak of the whole Waterloo Campaign has an interesting story. Benedetto Pistrucci was commissioned by the Prince Regent in 1819 to produce a medal for the four sovereigns responsible for the victory. He set to work and laboured for 30 years on a medal that would suit the sovereigns and their victory – 128mm in diameter.

The obverse has the busts of the Prince Regent, Alexander I of Russia, Francis II of Austria, and Fredrick William III of Prussia. On either side of them are Hercules and Justice. Above, the sun (or Apollo) drives a *quadriga*, preceded by the Dioscuri, while below Night rides in a *biga* attended by Furies and Fates.

The reverse has Wellington riding ahead with Blücher following. They are aided by Victory. Jupiter above in a *quadriga* throws thunderbolts at giants below. By 1849 when the medal was finished, only Wellington, out of those for whom the medal was intended, was still alive. The medal was never struck but in 1966 John Pinches produced a half size edition (64mm).

Napoleon spoke bold words to Joseph on 19 June, after Waterloo.

> All is not lost. I suppose that, when I reassemble my forces, I shall have 150,000 men. The *federes* and National Guards (such as are fit to fight) will provide 100,000 men, and the regimental depots another 50,000. I shall thus have 300,000 soldiers ready at once to bring against the enemy … There is still time to retrieve the situation. Write to me and tell me how the Chamber has been affected by this disastrous skirmish. I trust the deputies will realize that it is their duty at this crisis to stand by me and to help me to save France.[5]

The deputies, however, had other thoughts. They had done enough for Napoleon over fifteen years. A committee was formed, which on 25 June ordered him to leave Paris – which he did, going to Malmaison. A half-hearted attempt was made to place his son on the throne, as the small medallion (Br. 1667) suggests. Napoleon can have had no illusions about the outcome since the boy had been a prisoner in Vienna for a year.

Napoleon's intentions may be divined from a letter that Bertrand, Napoleon's Grand Marshal, wrote to Napoleon's librarian on the 25th.

> The Grand Marshal begs M. Barbier to be so good as to bring to La Malmaison tomorrow: (1) The list of ten thousand books and engravings, such as those of Denon's travels and the Egyptian Commission, of which the Emperor had several thousand copies. (2) Some works on America.[6]

In addition the Emperor wanted his travelling library 'brought up to date' and 'supplemented by a number of works on the United States'.

THE HUNDRED DAYS

Napoleon's plan was apparently to sail with Joseph to America – but the British had other plans. He left Malmaison on the 29th, reached Rochefort on 3 July and went on board one of the frigates reserved for him. But blocking the channel was a ship of the line, *Bellerophon*. Captain Maitland's orders were not to let Napoleon escape. After several days of waiting, Napoleon decided to place himself at the mercy of the British government. He wrote to the Prince Regent on 23 July.

> Your Royal Highness: victimized by the factions which divide my country, and by the hostility of the greatest European powers, I have ended my political career; and I come, as Themistocles did, to seat myself by the hearth of the British people. I put myself under the protection of its law – protection which I claim from Your Royal Highness, as the strongest, the stubbornest, and the most generous of my foes.[7]

On the morning of Saturday 15 July, Napoleon was piped aboard the *Bellerophon* and accorded full honours, but he appears to all observers a very small figure on the medal which pictures the mighty Bellerophon.

A medal in the Mudie series celebrates the final victory (Br. 1674). The Duke of Wellington appears on the obverse, the façade of the Louvre on the opposite face. The British Army entered Paris on 7 July 1815.

SURRENDER OF NAPOLEON. Napoleon surrenders to Captain Maitland on board the *Bellerophon*, 15 July 1815. (Brenet; Br. 1691)

THE DUKE OF WELLINGTON. The British Army enters Paris, 7 July 1815. The reverse shows the façade of the Louvre. (Br. 1674)

THE HUNDRED DAYS

The final word belongs to the French King, Louis XVIII, who benefited most from the Allies' victory. A medal by Andrieu (Br. 1724) expresses his gratitude for the faithfulness and devotion of the National Guard during the period of his exile. FIDELITE DEVOUEMENT appears with the king's bust on the obverse. On the reverse is a crowned five-pointed star encircling a *fleur-de-lis* and the following legend: '12th April, 3rd Mai 1814' and '19th March, 8th July'. 12 April was the date that the Count of Artois (the King's brother) entered Paris. The King arrived on 3 May. 19 March 1815 and 8 July mark the period of the King's second exile.

Notes

1. Rose, *Life of Napoleon I*, p.437.
2. Letter 21681.
3. Letter 21590.
4. *Le Moniteur*, May 21, 1815. I am indebted to David Bloch for the location of this reference and the translation.
5. J. M. Thompson, *Napoleon's Letters*, No. 290, p.307.
6. Thompson, No. 291, p.308.
7. Thompson, No. 292, p.309.

GRATITUDE OF THE KING. The King expresses his gratitude to the members of the Guard who have remained faithful to him during his exile. FIDELITE DEVOUEMENT appears with the bust of Louis XVIII on the obverse of this medal. The reverse has a crowned five-pointed star encircling a *fleur-de-lis* and a legend which gives the dates of the King's exile. (Andrieu; Br. 1724)

XX

The Legend

Napoleon's time on St Helena is the subject of two volumes by Norwood Young[1] and there are countless others; the Emperor has an enduring fascination for historians. As appealing as Napoleon was while in power in France, he appears to have become petty and mean – with occasional moments of grace – on St Helena. He does, however, respond to History, on a medal in the Mudie Series, which is 'inciting him to record those annals of his life which Fame … has already published.'[2] He manages, as history implores him, to portray his career in a favourable light for those who wished to see it as the one grand era in French history.

The death of Napoleon in 1821 is touchingly portrayed on a large medal in lead by Andrieu with St Helena as a rocky island in the sea and a ship with the setting sun; an eagle with a palm branch flies overhead. *IL MOURUT SUR UN ROCHER*, reads the legend. On the obverse, around a portrait of Napoleon arranged on a wreath, is a list of his principal victories. The return of Napoleon's remains to Paris in 1840 is commemorated on a medal showing his grave on St Helena.

Napoleon's original plan to sail to America was dependent on a British safe conduct. When that was not forthcoming he went on board the *Bellerophon* at Captain Maitland's invitation, placing himself 'under the protection of the laws of England'. He envisioned, it may be assumed, a life as an English gentleman in some quiet town on the English coast. It therefore came as a shock to find that he would be sent to St Helena as a prisoner, though that was a decision of the English government agreed upon by the Allied sovereigns, and one that was quite understandable considering his escape from his previous exile and the staggering loss of life at Waterloo that resulted. Napoleon however, saw it as evidence of English perfidy.

This betrayal was the theory that Napoleon cherished throughout his sojourn on St Helena. It is also the sentiment expressed by his advocates in the medal reproduced, if indeed the medal was struck after 1830. A copy in lead is said by his family to have been given to Sir Pulteney Malcolm, Naval Governor on St Helena 1816–17, by Napoleon. 'This family had had the piece in their possession for a great many years and there is no reason to suppose that the two medals

THE LEGEND

NAPOLEON ON ST HELENA (1815). Napoleon seated on a rock with head down. History on her knees urges him to take up the pen. Fame with a trumpet flies overhead. (Mills; Br. 1710)

THE DEATH OF NAPOLEON (1821). The island of St Helena with ships and the setting sun. An eagle with a palm branch flies overhead. *IL MOURUT SUR UN ROCHER*. (Andrieu; Br. 1844), lead, 69mm.

NAPOLEON'S MEDALS: *'Victory to the Arts'*

NAPOLEON'S REMAINS RETURNED TO PARIS (1840). Napoleon's grave on St Helena. (Bovy; Br. 1900)

NAPOLEON'S PROTEST AGAINST HIS EXILE Probably not struck until after the revolution of 1830, but the sentiments expressed are understandable in view of his letter to the Prince Regent. (Br. 1694)

concerned had not been presented to the ancestor [Sir Pulteney Malcolm] by Napoleon on St Helena.'³

It was determined, after Napoleon's departure to St Helena, that a statue of a national hero Henry IV was needed. The need was expressed even after Napoleon's first abdication. There were repeated pleas in *Le Moniteur* for money for the statue, but money was not the only requirement. Chaudet's statue of

TEXT OF THE PROTEST. 'I protest solemnly in the face of heaven and man against the violence that has been done to me … I presented myself in good faith to come and place myself under the protection of the laws of England … The faith of Britain has been lost in the hospitality of the *Bellerophon*. I appeal to history that says that an enemy who has fought twenty years in war against her people should come freely, in his misfortune, to seek asylum under her laws.' (Br. 1694), 51mm.

A COPY IN LEAD, MOUNTED IN IVORY of Br. 291, though of a slightly different strike. Said by Sir Pulteney Malcolm's family to have been given to him by Napoleon on St Helena. Malcolm was Naval Governor of St Helena from June 1816 to July 1817 and had many conversations with Napoleon. As Martin Howard points out in *Napoleon's Poisoned Chalice*, 'Malcolm had not been deliberately obstructive … but he had harboured rather more sympathy for Napoleon and had operated independently … to a greater degree than was proper for the Commander-in-Chief of a naval station.'

THE LEGEND

Napoleon on the column of the *Place Vendôme* was melted down, along with the despised statue of Desaix, resulting in the splendid equestrian statue of Henry IV (Br. 1753). France had turned her back on her Emperor.

Notes

1. Norwood Young, *Napoleon in Exile: St Helena, (1815–1821)*, 2 volumes, Philadelphia, John C. Winston Company. Also by Young, *Napoleon in Exile at Elba (1814–1815)*, 1914.
2. James Mudie, *An Historical and Critical Account of A Grand Series of National Medals*, London, 1820, p.145.
3. Laurence A. Brown, Managing Director, B.A. Seaby Limited.

THE STATUE OF HENRY IV (1817). Equestrian statue of Henry IV. There were repeated pleas in *Le Moniteur* for money for the statue. Chaudet's statue of Napoleon on top of the Column of the *Place Vendôme* was melted down for the metal to make it. (Andrieu; Br. 1753), 50mm.

Bibliography

Adani, Ettore, *Le Medaglie Napoleoniche Reguardanti L'Italia, 1796–1816*, Bologna: Forni Editore.

Babelon, Ernest, *Les médailles historiques de règne de Napoléon le Grande, Empereur et Roi*. New York: New York Numismatic Society, 1912.

Benoit, Francois, *L'Art Français sous la Révolution et l'Empire*, Paris: Société Française d'Editions d'Art, 1897.

Bramsem, L., *Médaillier Napoléon le Grand*, Paris: Alphonse Picard & Fils, 1904, 1907, 1913. Reprint, Hamburg: Peter Siemer, 1977, 3 volumes.

Brommer, Frank, *Heracles, The Twelve Labours of the Hero in Ancient Art and Literature*, New Rochelle: Aristide D. Caratzas, 1986.

Brunet, Marcelle, et Tamera Préaud, *Sèvres, Des origins à nos jours,* Fribourg, Switzerland, 1978.

Castelot, André, *King of Rome, A Biography of Napoleon's Tragic Son,* New York: Harper & Brothers, 1960.

Chandler, David G. *Dictionary of the Napoleonic Wars*, New York, 1979.

Chatelain, Jean, *Dominique Vivant Denon et le Louvre de Napoléon,* Paris: Librairie Académique Perrin, 1973.

Chevalier, Bernard, *Napoleon*, Memphis Exhibition Catalogue, Memphis, 1993.

De Caulaincourt, General, Duke of Vicenza, *With Napoleon in Russia, from the Original Memoirs,* New York: William Morrow, 1935.

De Fayolle, A. Evrard, *Recherches sur Bertrand Andrieu de Bordeaux,* Paris: Veuve Raymond Serrure, 1902.

Edwards, Edward, trans., *The Napoleonic Medals*, London: Henry, Hering, & Paul, 1837.

Esposito, General Vincent J. and Colonel John R. Elting, *A Military History and Atlas of the Napoleonic Wars, Revised edition,* London and Pennsylvania: Greenhill Books, 1999.

Fellman, George-Julien and M. Charles Lormant, *Trésor de Numismatique et de Glyptique,* Paris: Ritter et Doupil, 1836 and 1840.

Fontaine, Pierre-Francois-Leonard, *Journal, 1799–1853*, 2 volumes, Paris: Ecole Nationale Superiore, des Beaux-arts, 1987.

Forrer, L. ed., *Biographical Dictionary of Medallists*, 7 volumes, 1902–1923, New York: Burt Franklin (Reprint, 1970).

Glover, Michael, *The Napoleonic Wars*, New York: Hippocrene Books, 1878.

Goncourt, E. and J., *Histiore de la Société Française pendant le Directoire*. (Cited in Saunier, pp.36–37.)

Griffiths, Antony, 'The Design and Production of Napoleon's *Histoire Métallique*' *The Medal*, Spring 1990, pp.16–30.

—— 'The Origins of Napoleon's *Histoire Métallique*' *The Medal*, Autumn 1990, pp.28–38.

—— 'The End of Napoleon's *Histoire Métallique*' *The Medal*, Spring 1991, pp.34–49.

Guiffrey, J.J., 'La Monnaie des Médailles d'après les documents édit des Archives Nationales' *Revue Numismatique*, 3rd series, vol. IV. (1886).

BIBLIOGRAPHY

Haskell, Francis, and Nicholas Penny, *Taste and the Antique*, New Haven and London: Yale University Press, 1981.
Henin, M., *Histoire Numismatique de la Révolution Française*, Paris: J. S. Merlin, 1826.
Herold, J. Christopher, *The Age of Napoleon*, New York: Harper & Row, 1963.
—— *The Mind of Napoleon*, New York, 1955, 1961.
Hortense, la Reine, *Memoires de la Reine Hortense*, 3 volumes, Paris, 1927.
Howard, Martin, *Napoleon's Poisoned Chalice*, Stroud: The History Press, 2009.
Jones, Mark, *The Art of the Medal*, London: British Museum Publications, 1979.
Lanzac de Labourie, L., *Paris sous Napoléon – Spectacles et Musées*, Paris: Librairie Plon, 1913.
Laskey, Captain J.C., *A Description of the Series of Medals Struck at the National Medal Mint by Order of Napoleon Bonaparte*, London: H.R. Young, 1818.
Latimer, Elizabeth Wormley, (trans. & ed.), *Talks of Napoleon at St Helena, with General Baron Bourgaud*, Chicago: A.C. McClurg, & Co., 1903.
Lecestre, Léon, *Lettres Inédites de Napoléon I*, Paris: Librairie Plon, 1897.
Leith, James A., *The Idea of Art as Propaganda in France, 1750–1799*, Toronto: University of Toronto Press, 1964.
Lelièvre, Pierre, *Vivant Denon, Directeur des Beaux-Arts de Napoléon*, Paris: Librairie Floury, 1942.
Lloyd, Lady Mary, *New Letters of Napoleon I*, London: William Heinemann, 1898.
Maigne, M. *Journal Anecdotique de Mme Campan*, Paris: Baudouin Freres, Librairies, 1824.
Montagu, Violette M., *The Celebrated Madame Campan*, Philaedephia: J.B. Lippencott Company, 1914.
Nowinski, Judith, *Baron Dominique Vivant Denon (1745–1825)*, Cranbury, N.J.: Associated University Presses, 1970.
Reval, Gabrielle, *Madame Campan, Assistant de Napoléon*, Paris: Les Vies Authentiques, 1931.
Rose, John Holland, *The Life of Napoleon I*, 2 volumes, London: G. Bell and Sons Ltd., 1929.
Rosenberg, Pierre, and various authors, *Dominique-Vivant Denon, L'oeil de Napoléon*, Paris: Musée du Louvre, 1999.
Saunier, Charles, *Les Conquêtes Artistiques de la Révolution et de l'Empire*. Paris: Librairie Renouard, 1902.
Savary, Anne Jean Marie René, *Mémoires du duc de Rovigo*, 8 volumes. Paris: Boussange, 1828.
Scargill, Ann Mudie, *Medallic History of Napoleon Bonaparte Translated by Miss Ann Mudie Scargill from the Original Manuscript Intended to Have Been Published by the Late Government of France*, London: J. Shaw, 1820.
Schom, Alan, *Napoleon Bonaparte*, New York: Harper-Collins, 1997.
Thompson, J.M., *Napoleon Bonaparte, His Rise and Fall*, New York: Oxford University Press, 1951, 1969.
Thompson, J.M., ed., *Napoleon's Letters*, New York: E. p.Dutton & Co. Inc., 1934, 1954.
Uffindell, A., *Napoleon's Immortals*, Stroud: Spellmount, 2007.
Vauthier, G. 'Denon et le gouvernement des arts, sous le Consulate' *Annales revolutionaire*, 1911, pp.336–365.
Wescher, Paul,'Vivant Denon and the Musée Napoléon' *Apollo* Sept. 1964, pp.178–186.
Whitcomb, Edward A., *Napoleon's Diplomatic Service*, Durham: Duke University Press, 1979.
Wright, Constance, *Daughter to Napoleon*, New York: Holt, Rinehart and Winston, 1961.
Young, Norwood, *Napoleon in Exile at Elba (1814–1815)*, Philadelphia: Winston, 1914.
—— *Napoleon in Exile at St Helena (1815–1821)*, 2 volumes, Philadelphia: Winston, 1915.
Wilson, Sir Arthur, ed., *A Diary of St Helena, The Journal of Lady Malcolm (1816–1817)*, New York and London: Harper & Brothers, 1899.

Index of Medals

Br. 37 *Crossing the St Bernard*, 51
Br. 38 *Bonaparte at Marengo*, 86
Br. 40 *Battle of Marengo*, 85
Br. 42 *Cisalpine Republic Restored/Bonaparte*, 43, 150
Br. 44 *Death of Desaix at Marengo*, 86
Br. 57 *18 Brumaire*, 89
Br. 59 *Bonaparte at Lyons*, 87
Br. 61 *National Column*, 90, 91
Br. 64 *Column of the Department of the Seine*, 92
Br. 66 *Column of the Department of the Seine and Marne*, 93
Br. 68 *Foundation of the Quai Desaix*, 94
Br. 74 *Marengo – Keys of Captured Cities*, 84
Br. 77 *Assassination Attempt of December 1800*, 187
Br. 106 *Peace of Luneville/Bonaparte*, 52, 150
Br. 107 *Peace of Luneville/Bonaparte*, 96, 151
Br. 152 *Visit of the King and Queen of Etruria to Paris*, 97
Br. 167 *'Armed for Peace'*, 102
Br. 189 *Constitution of the Italian Republic at Lyons*, 100
Br. 195 *Peace of Amiens*, 47
Br. 200 *Return of Astree – Peace of Amiens/Bonaparte*, 99, 151
Br. 204 *Cornwallis at Amiens*, 98
Br. 213 *Reestablishment of Religion/Bonaparte*, 67, 152
Br. 214 *Organisation of Public Instruction/Bonaparte*, 62, 151
Br. 271 *Occupation of Hanover/The Treaty of Amiens Broken by England*, 50, 103
Br. 275 *A La Fortune Conservatrice/Bonaparte*, 183, 152
Br. 280 *Venus de Medici/Bonaparte*, 9, 153

Br. 291 *Giving of the Civil Code*, 17
Br. 310 *The Legion of Honour*, 202
Br. 318 *Legionary Honours/Plan of the Camp at Boulogne*, 104, 105
Br. 320 *Hercules ties up the Nemean Lion/Bonaparte*, 103, 158
Br. 326 *Coronation of Napoleon*, 108
Br. 329 *Small Coronation Medal*, 108
Br. 350 *Pope Pius VII at Paris*, 110
Br. 357 *Distribution of the Eagles*, 111
Br. 358 *Coronation Festivities/Bonaparte*, 113, 154
Br. 359 *The Imperial Eagle/Coronation Festivities*, 112
Br. 367 *Laocoon Gallery*, 13
Br. 370 *Apollo Gallery*, 13
Br. 400 *La Vaccine*, 18
Br. 418 *Iron Crown of the Lombards*, 114
Br. 420 *Coronation in Milan/Bonaparte*, 113, 155
Br. 422 *Liguria United to France*, 125
Br. 426 *Monument to Desaix*, 85
Br. 432 *Address on the Lech Bridge*, 117
Br. 442 *French Insignia Recovered*, 118
Br. 443 *Capture of Vienna and Pressburg*, 44
Br. 444 *The Capture of Vienna/Bonaparte*, 24, 155
Br. 445 *Battle of Austerlitz*, 52
Br. 446 *Battle of Austerlitz*, 119
Br. 452 *Meeting at Urshutz*, 120
Br. 453 *Fame Blows her Trumpet*, 116
Br. 455 *Peace of Pressburg*, 140
Br. 460 *Venice Returned to Italy*, 123
Br. 461 *Te Deum Sung in St Stephen's Cathedral*, 121
Br. 463 *Column of the Grand Army*, 15
Br. 467 *The School of Medicine*, 61
Br. 476 *The Empress Josephine*, 162
Br. 512 *Istria Conquered*, 122

INDEX OF MEDALS

Br. 513 *Dalmatia Conquered*, 122
Br. 516 *Conquest of Naples*, 124
Br. 522 *Marriage of the Prince of Baden*, 127
Br. 527 *The Grand Sanhedrin*, 68
Br. 537 *Battle of Jena*, 129
Br. 538 *Napoleon as Jupiter*, 130
Br. 546 *Entry into Berlin*, 130
Br. 551 *Alliance with Saxony*, 128
Br. 553 *Sovereignties Given*, 125
Br. 554 *Napoleon as Hercules*, 40
Br. 557 *Carrousel Arch*, 14
Br. 620 *French Army on the Vistula*, 54
Br. 628 *Battle of Eylau*, 132
Br. 631 *Napoleon at Osterode*, 132
Br. 632 *Battle of Friedland*, 134
Br. 633 *Victory inscribes a Shield at Friedland*, 134
Br. 635 *Conquest of Silesia*, 135
Br. 640 *The Three Sovereigns at Tilsit*, 144
Br. 660 *Creation of the Kingdom of Westphalia*, 137
Br. 662 *Marriage of Jérôme Napoleon/ Bonaparte*, 138, 154
Br. 634 *Campaigns of 1806–1807*, 138
Br. 679 *Napoleon and Diogenes*, 48
Br. 689 *Simplon Pass*, 58
Br. 690 *Road from Nice to Rome*, 60
Br. 767 *Hortense*, 163
Br. 770 *Pauline*, 164
Br. 772 *Caroline*, 165
Br. 776 *Elisa*, 166
Br. 844 *Treaty of Pressburg Broken by Austria/Abensberg and Eckmuhl*, 41, 142
Br. 846 *Battle of Ratisbon/Bonaparte*, 142, 157
Br. 847 *Entry into Vienna*, 143
Br. 848 *Reunion of France and Italy*, 54
Br. 849 *Rome and Paris*, 145
Br. 854 *French Eagles Beyond the Raab*, 55
Br. 859 *Battle of Essling/Crossing the Danube*, 56
Br. 860 *Battle of Wagram*, 44
Br. 862 *Battle of Wagram/Bonaparte*, 51, 156
Br. 868 *The Ourcq Canal*, 60
Br. 870 *Jupiter Stator/English attack on Antwerp*, 23, 144
Br. 876 *Peace of Vienna*, 144
Br. 879 *Conquest of Illyria*, 19
Br. 939 *Visit of the King and Queen of Bavaria to the Medal Mint*, 145
Br. 943 *Marriage in Vienna*, 169

Br. 949 *Arrival at Strasbourg*, 170
Br. 952 *Marriage of Napoleon and Marie Louise*, 171
Br. 954 *Marriage of Napoleon and Marie Louise*, 171
Br. 956 *Marriage of Napoleon and Marie Louise*, 172
Br. 961 *Napoleon and Marie Louise/ Hymen Chasing Mars*, 172, 173
Br. 976 *Statue of Desaix*, 93
Br. 980 *Orphelines de la Legion D'Honneur*, 63
Br. 1094 *The King of Rome/The King of Rome and the Roman Wolf*, 175, 176
Br. 1099 *Marie Louise as a Roman Matron*, 175
Br. 1100 *Napoleon and Marie Louise of Austria/The King of Rome*, 168, 182
Br. 1108 *The Baby Hercules*, 45
Br. 1125 *Baptism of the King of Rome*, 177
Br. 1138 *Wellington as Fabius Cunctator*, 133
Br. 1156 *Taking of Wilna*, 189
Br. 1158 *French Eagle on the Borysthenes*, 58
Br. 1162 *Battle of Moscow/Bonaparte*, 44, 158
Br. 1166 *French Army on the Volga*, 58
Br. 1168 *Retreat from Russia*, 57, 189
Br. 1178 *French School of Fine Art in Rome/Bonaparte*, 66, 158
Br. 1223 *Monument on Mount Cenis*, 191
Br. 1229 *Battle of Lützen/Bonaparte*, 159, 190
Br. 1232 *Battle of Wurtchen*, 191
Br. 1259 *Battle of Leipzig*, 192
Br. 1273 *Battle of Hanau*, 193
Br. 1303 *Marie Louise of Austria*, 36, 163
Br. 1333 *Napoleon Leaves from St Cloud*, 178
Br. 1365 *Fortune Adverse*, 184
Br. 1386 *Napoleon Abdicates*, 194
Br. 1406 *Landing of Louis XVIII at Calais/Louis XVIII Welcomed by France*, 28, 198
Br. 1415 *To Elba*, 195
Br. 1441 *Repose of Hercules*, 45
Br. 1464 *History (or Victory) Writing on a Tablet/Stay of Alexander I in Paris*, 196, 197
Br. 1465 *The Emperor Francis Visits the Mint*, 119
Br. 1466 *Frederick William III, King of Prussia, Visits the Mint*, 196

Br. 1482 *A Crowned Eagle Flying with the Original Legion of Honour in its Beak*, 201
Br. 1489 *The Duke of Cambridge/The British Re-enter Hanover*, 199
Br. 1550 *Vaccinations at Paris*, 22
Br. 1590 *The Gulf of Juan – Monument*, 203
Br. 1591 *Return of Napoleon*, 204
Br. 1632 *The Field of May*, 205
Br. 1664 *Napoleon gives his Son to France/Bonaparte*, 181, 159
Br. 1667 *'Proclaimed Emperor of the French'/The King of Rome*, 180
Br. 1674 *The Duke of Wellington*, 210
Br. 1691 *Surrender of Napoleon*, 209
Br. 1694 *Napoleon's Protest Against his Exile*, 214, 215
Br. 1710 *Napoleon on St Helena*, 213
Br. 1724 *Gratitude of the King*, 211
Br. 1753 *The Statue of Henry IV*, 217
Br. 1844 *Death of Napoleon/Bonaparte*, 213, 159
Br. 1990 *Napoleon's Remains Returned to Paris/Bonaparte*, 214, 160
Br. 1906 *Restoration of the Statue of Napoleon*, 29
Br. 2188 *Struck in London, 1804*, 43
C.H. Kuchler *Last Farewell of Louis XVI*, 32
Donadio *Vivant Denon*, 16
Essling 769 *Bonaparte in Egypt – the Legend*, 81
Forrer *Minting Press*, 36

H. 23 *Siege of the Bastille*, 30
H. 59 *National Assembly – Abandonment of Privileges*, 30
H. 62 *Arrival of the King in Paris*, 31
H. 363 *Paris Commune – Attack on the Tuileries*, 31
H. 376 *Battle for the Bridge at Lodi*, 74
H. 731 *Battle of Montenotte/Gayrard*, 73, 148
H. 744 *Castglione and Peschiera*, 75
H. 767 *'Buonaparte, General in Chief of the Brave Italian Army'*, 147
H. 773 *Hercules Slays the Hydra – Battles of Millesimo and Dego*, 41
H. 782 *Capitulation of Mantua*, 76
H. 785 *Surrender of Mantua*, 46
H. 787 *Passage of the Tagliamento*, 55
H. 789 *Council of the Ancients – Constitution of the Year III*, 32
H. 811 *Treaty of Campoformio/General Bonaparte*, 11, 148
H. 812 *Bonaparte as Italicus/Alexander Bonaparte*, 10, 71
H. 816 *Bust of Bonaparte/Minerva*, 149
H. 850 *Conquest of Lower Egypt*, 53, 81
H. 857 *Virtute Nihil Obstat & Armis*, 80
H. 879 *Conquest of Egypt/Bonaparte*, 81
H. 896, *Conquest of Upper Egypt*, 22, 81
H. 921 *Arrival at Frejus/The Roman God, Bonus Eventus*, 185, 186
Mudie 7 *Syria Saved; Bonaparte Repulsed*, 82
Waterloo Medal, 206, 207

Index

Aboukir, Battle of, 79
Alexander I, Emperor of Russia, 65, 118, 134–7, 188, 197, 208
Amiens, Peace of/Treaty of, 33, 46–7, 50–1, 96, 98–9, 101, 103, 151
Andrieu, Bertrand, 15–16, 17–19, 21, 28, 30–1, 33, 44, 54, 60, 62, 67, 85, 96, 119–21, 125, 127–9, 131–2, 135–8, 140–1, 143–7, 149, 151–2, 154, 159–64, 167–8, 170, 174, 177, 182, 189, 196–7, 204, 211–13, 217
Appiani, Andrea, 32, 41, 43, 46, 55, 72, 75, 86, 149, 186–7
Austerlitz, Battle of, 29, 37, 52, 78, 105, 115-6, 118–21, 123, 125, 140, 194, 202
Austria, 15, 43, 44, 52, 72, 73, 76, 96, 105, 115, 119, 120, 123, 140, 141, 144–146, 163, 168, 181, 208

de Beauharnais, Josephine, 64, 98, 109, 112, 131, 135, 161–164, 174, 200
Bergeret, Pierre, 32–3, 48, 128, 130, 142
Bonaparte, Caroline, 4, 164, 165
Bonaparte, Elisa, 59, 164, 166, 167, 181
Bonaparte, Jérôme, 33, 128, 135, 138, 139, 154
Bonaparte, Joseph 98, 124–5, 209
Bonaparte, Hortense, 64, 161–163, 219
Bonaparte, Lucien, 79, 84, 88, 91, 94–5
Bonaparte, Napoléon Francis Joseph Charles, King of Rome, 43, 45, 52, 161, 174–81, 205
Bonaparte, Pauline, 64, 125, 162, 164
Borodino, Battle of, 43, 188
Bovy, Antoine, 81, 83, 160, 214
Brenet, Nicolas, 14–17, 33–4, 36, 38, 53–4, 56, 68, 79, 81–2, 85–6, 93, 112, 115–6, 118, 120–5, 132, 134, 137, 142, 150, 153–4, 159–60, 163, 165–6, 171, 178–9, 181, 183–4, 190–2, 194, 198, 209

Campoformio, Peace of/Treaty of, 10–11, 50, 71–2, 76, 149
Catholic Church, 67, 69
Chaudet, Antoine-Denis, 15, 17–21, 28–9, 32, 37–8, 44, 50, 52, 54, 93, 95, 104, 108, 120, 134, 147, 149, 154, 160, 215, 217
Chavanne, Jean Marie, 72, 87, 149
Cisalpine Republic, 41, 43, 86, 98, 100, 150, 185, 186
Confederation of the Rhine, 127–8, 141–2

Danube, the, 55, 56, 141, 143, 188
Denon, Vivant, 8–10, 14–18, 20–1, 24, 29, 31, 33–5, 37–8, 59, 69, 91, 108–9, 115–19, 121, 123–4, 131, 143–4, 156, 161, 168, 171, 190–1, 196
Desaix, Louis Charles Antoine, 85, 86, 88, 93–95, 217
Droz, Jean-Pierre, 33–4, 36, 41, 43–5, 52, 96, 98–9, 103, 110, 136, 147, 149–51, 154, 156–8
Dumarest, Rambert, 33, 47
Duvivier, Pierre Simon Benjamin, 11–12, 16, 31, 50, 77, 88, 90, 148–9

Egypt, 5, 12, 21–2, 78–81, 83–4, 153, 185
Elba, 105, 164, 174, 179, 194–5, 201, 203–4
England, 33, 41, 47, 52, 68, 70, 7 8–80, 78, 79, 80, 96, 98, 101, 103–106, 117, 130, 183, 212, 215
English Channel, 101, 105, 116, 209
Essling, Battle of, 55–6, 69, 141, 188, 202
Eylau, Battle of, 129, 131–2, 202

Fragonard, Alexandre-Everiste, 32, 44, 51, 55–6, 60, 81, 84, 125
Frederick Augustus, Elector of Saxony, 128
Frederick William, III, King of Prussia, 130, 136, 194, 196
Friedland, Battle of, 33, 48, 131–2, 134, 202

Florence, 9, 190
Francis I of Austria/Francis II, Holy Roman Emperor, 115, 118–21, 181, 191, 194, 208

Galle, Andre, 22, 33, 38, 44, 48, 57, 115–16, 130, 154, 171, 175–6, 185–6, 189
Gatteaux, Edouard, 66, 75–6, 91, 157–8
Gatteaux, Nicolas, 16, 31, 66, 157
Gayrard, Raymond, 33, 59–60, 119, 148, 194, 196

Hanau, Battle of, 192–3
Hanover, 50–1, 101, 137, 198–9
Heliopolis, Battle of, 79
Henrionnet, 179–80
Hercules, 19, 20, 40, 41, 43–45, 71, 73, 86, 101, 103, 105, 117, 129, 143, 157, 158, 174, 186, 188, 206, 208

Italy, 10, 12, 13, 17, 43, 45, 51, 52, 54, 59, 71–74, 76, 79, 84–86, 88, 96, 113, 114, 121, 123, 125, 128, 141, 147, 149, 154, 156, 166, 172, 173, 181, 185, 190, 191

Jena, Battle of, 33, 37, 48, 120, 128–30, 202
Jeuffroy, Romain-Vincent, 9, 33, 43, 50, 73, 103–4, 108, 111–13, 153, 154
Jews, 68–69
Jouannin, Julien Marie, 153, 171, 174–5
Jupiter, 21, 23, 24, 28, 37, 40, 48, 118, 121, 122, 130, 141, 143, 144, 207, 208

Lavy, Carlo Michele, 32, 41, 43, 46, 55, 72, 75–6, 86, 149–50
Legion of Honour, 63–4, 104–5, 201–2
Leipzig, Battle of, 192
Louis XVIII, King of France, 8, 28, 105, 157, 158, 161, 193, 201, 202, 211
Luneville, Peace of/Treaty of, 33, 52, 96, 150–1
Lützen, Battle of, 159, 188, 190–1, 202
Lyons, 33, 72, 84, 86–7, 100, 149, 179, 204–7

Manfredini, Luigi, 24, 32, 34, 51, 100, 113, 117, 141–2, 154–7, 172–3, 186–8
Marengo, Battle of, 32, 41, 43, 51, 79, 84–8, 93, 131, 134, 186, 204
Marie Louise, Empress of the French, 145, 161, 163, 165, 171–175, 177–179, 181, 182, 192
Mars, 14, 28, 45–47, 66, 75, 93 97, 98, 105, 111, 131, 134, 173, 192, 205

Medal Mint, 14, 16–17, 29, 34, 38, 47, 69, 79, 83, 109, 115, 119, 145, 161, 170, 194, 196–7
Milan, 24, 26, 32, 34, 43, 71–2, 76–7, 88, 113–14, 128, 149, 154–5, 173, 190–1
Montenotte, Battle of, 48, 72–3, 148–9
Montmirail, Battle of, 192, 200
Moscow, Battle of, 44, 158, 188
Murat, Joachim, 115, 116, 125, 164, 165

Naples, 10, 34, 121, 124–5, 129, 164, 165
Nelson, Horatio, 79, 80
Nile, Battle of the, 80–1

Ourcq Canal, 60–1

Paris, Peace of/Treaty of, 45
Place Vendôme, 15, 33, 37, 65, 88, 90, 93, 95, 129, 217
Pressburg, Peace of/Treaty of, 14–15, 43–4, 117, 120–5, 140–2
Prudhon, Pierre Paul, 21–3, 112–13, 137–8
Prussia, 128, 130, 136, 194, 196, 208
Pyramids, Battle of the, 79, 81, 83

Ratisbon, Battle of, 142, 157
Rhine, the, 127, 128
Rome, 10–11, 14–15, 25, 33, 37, 44–5, 52, 59, 60, 66, 68, 72, 97, 120, 129, 137, 144–6, 157–8, 161, 166, 174–82, 190, 205, 218
Russia, 52, 57, 58, 64, 65, 115, 136, 138, 188, 189, 197, 208, 218

St Cloud, 177–8, 192
St Helena, 40, 160, 186, 212–16
Seine, the, 60, 61, 86, 90–93, 115
Spain, 96, 97

Tilsit, Peace of/Treaty of, 134–6
Trafalgar, Battle of, 105

Ulm, Battle of, 48, 115–6, 202

Venus, 9, 16, 18, 19, 61, 150, 162
Vienna, Peace of/Treaty of, 144
Volga, the, 53, 58, 181

Wagram, Battle of, 43–4, 51, 55–6, 143, 156, 202
Waterloo, Battle of, 44, 174, 179, 206, 208, 212
Wellington, Duke of, 44, 131, 133, 205, 207–10
Wurtchen, Battle of, 188, 190–1